SCHOOLING
FOR
SOCIAL DIVERSITY
An Analysis of Policy and Practice

SCHOOLING
FOR
SOCIAL DIVERSITY

An Analysis of Policy and Practice

ROBERT C. SEROW
North Carolina State University

Teachers College, Columbia University
New York and London 1983

Published by Teachers College Press, 1234 Amsterdam Avenue, New York, N.Y. 10027

Library of Congress Cataloging in Publication Data

Serow, Robert C., 1947–
　Schooling for social diversity.

　Bibliography: p.
　Includes index.
　1.　Educational sociology—United States.
2.　School integration—United States. 3.　Educational
equalization—United States. 4.　Minorities—Education—United States. 5.　Handicapped children
—Education—United States. I.　title.
LC191.4.S47　1983　　　370.19　　　82-10709

ISBN 0-8077-2729-6

Manufactured in the United States of America

88　87　86　85　84　83　　　1　2　3　4　5　6

To
D.G.S.
and
K.A.O.

Contents

Preface

One of the clearest trends in the recent history of American education has been the increasing importance of social policies and programs within the public schools. In addition to carrying out their traditional academic mission, the schools have been asked to achieve racial integration, to help low-income children overcome their initial social and economic disadvantages, to promote support for cultural diversity, and to absorb large numbers of handicapped children into regular classrooms. These programs have been costly, not only in terms of finances, but also in the investment of time, energy, and effort by educators and students. Not suprisingly, there has sometimes been considerable controversy over the merits of specific programs. But what is most noteworthy about these policies is the assumption on which they are based—that public schools can and should be used as an instrument of wholesale social reform. Moreover, the changes they seek fall within one of the most sensitive areas of American life. Specifically, each of these policies aims quite directly at the integration of racial or other minority groups into the nation's institutional mainstream.

In attempting to foster social integration, these programs have also addressed a number of other objectives. One of these is the promotion of tolerance for diversity, that is, the individual's willingness to accept the substantial social, cultural, and political diversity found within the nation's population. While tolerance has long been a major goal of American education, the policy innovations of the past few decades have increased its importance.

This book examines the contributions of contemporary public schools to the socialization of tolerance. The literature to date has seldom provided a unified, systematic treatment of this topic. Instead, research and theory have focused on single components of this process. Thus, the important connections that exist between racial desegregation and political socialization have been overlooked, as have the linkages between each of these and the most recent social programs. As a result, policymaking has been little informed by previous successes and failures.

The progression of this volume is from an exploration of past experiences to an analysis of current trends. Chapter 1 introduces the concept of social diversity, and illustrates the ways in which heterogeneous societies, particularly the United States, have attempted to deal with the consequences of a diverse population. While the American experience has been one of inconsistency and change, one recurring factor has been the role of education, and particularly public education, in bridging gaps between groups and in fostering social integration. Two major types of tolerance socialization carried on by the schools—the inculcation of democratic political norms and the improvement of racial relations—are reviewed in detail in chapter 2. From these reviews, it is concluded that surprisingly little is known about the means by which public education promotes tolerance for diversity. Chapter 3 spells out some of the shortcomings in existing research and theory, and offers an alternative interpretation of the school's role. Of particular importance is the success of desegregated public schools in shaping students' capacity for tolerant behavior, an outcome that has generally received little attention in the prior literature. In chapter 4 I show how this approach can be pursued in studies of intergroup relations in the schools.

The focus of the final sections of the book shifts to current policies and trends. Chapters 5 and 6 deal with two of the most controversial issues in public education today: mainstreaming the handicapped and multicultural education. In the last chapter, I speculate on education in the 1980s, and especially the effects that shifting budgetary priorities and social beliefs may have on the tolerance mission of public schools.

A book of this nature poses challenges for the author and perhaps for some readers as well. The primary tasks for the author are to synthesize vast amounts of research evidence and theory from several different fields, and to place them within a coherent framework. For example, how much—and which types—of information should be included to provide necessary background without engulfing the reader in a sea of technical detail? The interdisciplinary approach of this volume may also present obstacles to readers. In an age of increasing specialization, some readers may intend to concentrate on a particular policy area or line of research. Yet, one central theme of this book is the interrelatedness of all school practices that aim at increasing tolerance for diversity. To a considerable degree, each section and each chapter builds on points made previously; I hope that the connections among all topics become clear in due course.

Finally, many of the existing books and articles on the matters addressed here have taken the form of practitioners' guides, and are replete with very specific recommendations for improving teaching, counseling, or administration in the schools. This is less true of the present volume, which approaches the socialization of tolerance more from the perspective of social science than of pedagogy. However, it is obvious that school programs should not be formulated without a decent understanding of their social and political ramifications. For this reason, it is hoped that this book will prove timely and useful to those who actually carry out the work of tolerance socialization.

There are many individuals who, in one way or another, have shared in the creation of this book. Emil Haller, Daniel

Solomon, Kenneth Strike, and Carl Dolce have provided valuable insights and experience in the matters discussed here, and have also read and commented on earlier drafts of several chapters. The enduring influence of Robin M. Williams is best evidenced in the frequency with which his work on intergroup relations is cited throughout this volume. At North Carolina State University, colleagues and students have provided advice and encouragement. Finally, Brenda Mills, Barbara Scott, Leigh Ann Watts, and Karen Rolin have painstakingly deciphered and typed several versions of the manuscript.

SCHOOLING
FOR
SOCIAL DIVERSITY

An Analysis of Policy and Practice

1

Diversity and Its Consequences

By virtually any measure, the United States is one of the most diverse societies on the face of the earth. Numerous factors have contributed to the population mix, including settlement patterns in the colonial era, the importation of African slaves, the conquest of vast amounts of territory belonging to Native Americans and Mexicans, the need for a greatly expanded labor force during the period of industrialization, and the attractiveness of the relatively fluid economic and political systems. Today, the American population includes broad cross sections of many of the racial, ethnic, linguistic, and religious groups known to humankind (see Table 1-1).

Beyond their ethnic and religious diversity, Americans can be grouped or sorted along countless other lines as well. One type of collectivity that is particularly common in the United States is the *voluntary association*. In an early commentary on this point, the French scholar-journalist Alexis de Tocqueville observed that "in no country in the world has the principle of association been more successfully used, or more unsparingly applied to a multitude of different objects than in America."[1] To this day, Americans remain a nation of joiners, who often

1

TABLE 1.1: Selected Aspects of Racial, Religious, and Ethnic Diversity in the United States

ETHNICITY		RACE	
British	25,993,000	White	188,341,000
German	20,517,000	Black	26,488,000
Irish	12,240,000	Native American	1,418,195
Hispanic	14,606,000	Asian	3,501,000
Italian	7,101,000		
French	3,939,000	RELIGION	
Polish	3,686,000		
Russian	1,747,00	Protestant	73,704,000
		Roman Catholic	49,602,000
		Jewish	5,781,000
		Eastern Churches (mainly Orthodox)	3,632,000
		Other	1,029,000

SOURCE: Compiled from U.S., Bureau of the Census, *Statistical Abstract of the United States: 1979*, 100th ed. (Washington, D.C.: U.S., Bureau of the Census, 1979), tables 35 and 39; "The New Population Mix," *New York Times*, 6 September 1981; C. Jacquet, ed. *Yearbook of American and Canadian Churches, 1980* (Nashville: Abingdon, 1980), table 1-F.

NOTE: Statistics on Hispanics and on racial groups are based on provisional data from the 1980 census; estimates of ethnic and religious affiliation are based on 1973 and 1978 data, respectively.

find satisfaction and purpose by affiliating with others within the framework of an organization. According to one source, there were no fewer than 13,273 nationally chartered, non-profit associations active in the United States in 1979,[2] ranging in purpose, influence, and visibility from the American Federation of Labor and Congress of Industrial Organizations (14,300,000 members) to the North American Blueberry Council (6,000), the Committee to End Pay Toilets in America (1,600), and the War of 1812 Society (1,000).[3] In addition to the voluntary association, Americans (as well as other peoples) share memberships in other types of collectivities. Certainly the most familiar of these is the small, intimate aggregation known as the *primary group*. As exemplified by the family, primary groups are characterized by a relatively low degree of formal structure and by a fairly wide range of general purposes and functions. Families thus have a "flatter" hierarchy, in which children are subordinate (at least theoretically) to their parents, than do other types of organizations. Also, in contrast to voluntary associations, families typically do not exist in order to attain any single, precisely defined objective. Rather, the family's functions are diffuse, and indeed can be said to include almost anything that is not specifically discharged by other groups.

While each of these types of groups has an important influence on the behavior of its members, the present discussion will focus primarily on yet another type of collectivity—the *social category*. Here, we are talking about individuals who share some personal characteristic that sets them apart from other members of society. Usually, the distinctive characteristic is physical (e.g., race), cultural (religion or ideology), or a combination of both (ethnicity), although some specific types of behavior may also qualify individuals for separate status (e.g., homosexuality).[4] The significance of any of these characteristics varies greatly over time and place, and, in general, it remains unclear why a certain trait or feature is singled out as particularly distinctive. What does seem certain, however, is that such differentiation is somehow related to the basic values and beliefs of the group in question. Thus, a group whose members initially differ from outsiders on fundamental values will come to be seen as a breed apart. Conversely, the perception that a group's values are distinct from those of the mainstream may arise simply because its members differ from outsiders in some other respect. Social categories, then, are what sociologists usually have in mind when they speak of the diversity of a population. In the case of the United States, the most important bases for social categorization are race and, to a somewhat lesser extent, ethnicity.

RACIAL AND ETHNIC DIFFERENTIATION

As generally used within the social scientific literature, race and ethnicity are related but conceptually distinct terms. Pierre van den Berghe has pointed out that ethnicity is sometimes treated as the more inclusive term, and is used to describe any group (or its descendants) that is characterized by territorial clustering, endogamy (marriage within the group), and a common language.[5] From this perspective, race may be viewed as a special instance of ethnicity, insofar as it describes an ethnic group that is also marked by distinctive physiological characteristics, for example, skin color, hair texture, or facial features. However, as social categories, race and ethnicity become significant only if group membership is accompanied by a consciousness of a distinction between members and nonmembers, "ins" and "outs," "us" and "them."[6] Thus, racial and ethnic differentiation has both objective (language, territoriality, endogamy, physiology) and subjective (group consciousness) components.

In recent years, several writers have cautiously advanced the proposition that the tendency to emphasize group distinctiveness is deeply rooted in human nature, and is thus not merely a product of specific social, political, and economic circumstances, as has often been thought to be the case. Van den Berghe, for instance, calls attention to a sociobiological explanation for racism and ethnocentrism, namely, that social behavior is influenced by one's genetic links to other individuals. The closer the ties, the more positive the interactions, and conversely. Since racial and ethnic groups are characteristically endogamous, their members have closer genetic links to insiders than to outsiders, and can be expected to show a fairly high level of within-group solidarity and preference. "In other words, ethnocentrism, nepotism, tribalism, nationalism, sectarianism, parochialism, [and] racism . . . are biologically selected because they contribute to the actor's inclusive fitness."[7] Along similar lines, Gordon hypothesizes that human beings are essentially narcissistic, and act primarily out of self-interest. Since ethnicity (or race) is an integral part of the self, intergroup relations are shaped by interests, passions, and concerns comparable to those engendered by the pursuit of the individual's immediate self-interest.[8] Hence, "man defending the honor or welfare of his ethnic group is man defending himself."[9]

In many of the more advanced industrialized nations, racial and ethnic factors have assumed a growing importance over the past few decades. Part of the explanation appears to lie in the increasing heterogeneity of those societies, which has resulted primarily from immigration from Third World nations. For example, the urban riots that occurred in Great Britain during the summer of 1981 called attention to that nation's relatively sudden shift from a racially homogeneous population to one that now has significant black and Asian minorities. Additionally, the development of mass media has made possible the dissemination of news and information about certain ethnic, racial, and religious movements, thereby heightening minority-group consciousness across the world.[10] Moreover, the very nature of modern industrial society itself seems to contribute to the formation of racial/ethnic awareness. Several observers have suggested that the emergence of complex, impersonal forms of social organization in place of more traditional structures has created in many individuals a loss of self-identity, which is compensated for by a renewed interest in one's racial or ethnic origins or religious affiliation. Thus, subgroups provide "a sense of belongingness and quality of self-esteem"[11] that may be otherwise unavailable. In this sense, group identification serves a largely symbolic purpose. However, race and ethnicity are also believed to have important political and economic functions, especially in the United States. According to some political theorists, the American system of government encourages the formation of interest groups. While the exact nature of the government's role as broker, referee, or pawn of interest blocs remains the subject of debate,[12] it does seem entirely predictable that racial and ethnic minorities would adopt the associational strategies traditionally employed by industrial organizations, labor unions, and other interest groups. Based on the proposition that there is strength in numbers, individuals who share some common background characteristic band together, attempt to raise the consciousness of other group members, and seek to influence the policies of government and other institutions. In short, ethnicity serves as a vehicle for asserting claims against society at large,[13] and as a means for "getting one's share."[14]

Clearly, social categories serve important functions within modern nation-states. Nevertheless, just as these groups bring together otherwise isolated individuals in pursuit of common goals, so too do they tend to separate their members from other individuals and groups, and thereby increase the prospects for divisiveness within society as a whole. In fact, sociologists generally believe that a truly heterogeneous nation is likely to be characterized by instability, tension, and internal conflict. According to the traditional thinking:

> A stable and orderly society calls for a population that is relatively homogeneous . . . [and that] shares widespread consensus on basic values and goals. Such conditions can best be achieved, sociologists believe, when the population is relatively homogeneous in religious, racial, ethnic, and national origins. The more heterogeneous the people of a society are in these regards, the more likely it is that they will disagree on interests, standards, goals, and values, and that conflict and disorder will ensue.[15]

In order to survive, therefore, heterogeneous societies must devise some system of intergroup relations that counteracts or overcomes the potential for disintegration that inheres within a racially or ethnically diverse population. In recent history, such arrangements have taken a variety of forms. In the interests of convenience, however, we may consider four basic models. One fairly common approach is characterized by the total *domination* of a single group, as in the case of South Africa, where whites enjoy nearly complete control over the legal, political, and police power of the state and over the private sector of the economy as well. Here, the subjugated group is isolated from meaningful participation in the social mainstream. As a result, its deviance from the standard or dominant culture has little consequence for the stability of the system as a whole, as long as the subordinate population is tightly controlled by the ruling group. A somewhat more subtle form of domination involves the gradual *assimilation* of minorities into the way of life of one group. Under these circumstances, less-powerful groups abandon distinctive cultural patterns and adopt those of the dominant element of society in order to gain the political, economic, and social rewards available only to "first-class" citizens. In a variation of this approach, society functions as a *melting pot,* in which the mainstream culture gradually evolves from the contributions of initially diverse groups. Here, too, minorities are absorbed into the social fabric by surrendering their distinctive ways of life, but the element of overt oppression of some groups by others is thought to be absent. Finally, a *pluralistic* society is one that tolerates, and in some cases encourages, social and cultural diversity. Although pluralism may be marked by some degree of isolation or separatism among groups, in its ideal form it provides a basis for peaceful, cooperative coexistence, and hence social integration.[16]

There exists little agreement as to which of these models best describes the American experience. At various times, and to varying degrees, intergroup relations in the United States have been characterized by domination (for instance, of blacks by whites), assimilation (into a predominantly Anglo-Saxon culture), the melting pot (following upon the massive European immigration in the late nineteenth and early twentieth centuries), and cultural pluralism (as now appears to be the fashion). However, at least with respect to *racial* relations, the United States has been depicted as a "herrenvolk democracy," insofar as the principles of democratic and cultural pluralism, which are thought to be the cornerstones of the "American way of life," have traditionally been reserved for the dominant racial group, that is, whites.[17] According to van den Berghe, white Americans, until quite recently, have resolved the inherent conflict between their constitutional ideals of freedom, justice, and equality and their outright oppression of blacks and other racial minorities by regarding nonwhites as something less than fully human. Indeed, by one congressional formula in the period preceding the Civil War, black slaves were held to be precisely three-fifths human. (For census purposes, five slaves were to be considered the equivalent of three whites.) By regarding blacks and Native Americans as something other than human beings, white Americans were able to permit the practices of slavery, segregation, and various other forms of racial oppression, while also maintaining their avowed support for democratic governance. Only in the years since World War II, van den Berghe suggests, has the United States abandoned herrenvolk democracy, and begun to move toward a somewhat more equalitarian, albeit highly competitive, system of race relations.

In addition to its troubled racial past, the United States has seen numerous other episodes of ethnic and cultural oppression. In opposition to the popular melting-pot theory, some critics have argued that the dominant American culture is essentially that of the Anglo-Saxons, and that ethnic, as well as racial, minorities have been forced to conform to the values, beliefs, and behavioral patterns of that group. Much of the current support for multicultural education, for example, comes from proponents of pluralism who charge that the "Anglo conformity" model has resulted in subtle but systematic discrimination against white and nonwhite ethnic minorities.[18] Furthermore, despite the guarantees of religious freedom set forth in the First Amendment, it might be argued that freedom of worship in the United States operates within relatively narrow boundaries. R. P. Wolff, for one, has suggested that the principle of religious toleration applies more to established faiths (Protestantism, Catholicism, and Judaism) than to sects that are perceived to be beyond the denominational mainstream.[19] Similarly, with respect to political diversity, American history is replete with instances, such as the "Red Raids" of the 1920s and "McCarthyism" thirty years later, in which radical groups and their suspected followers were denied basic civil liberties.

Nevertheless, the fact remains that for all of its problems, the United States has remained intact and relatively tolerant of at least certain forms of human diversity for most of its history. As Brant has noted, the Founding Fathers' elaboration of a code of personal liberties (both procedural and substantive) within a written constitution represented an achievement unparalleled in human experience up to that time.[20] Since then, the original guarantees of civil rights and civil liberties have been considerably broadened through several types of action. First, the Constitution has been amended to extend full citizenship status to blacks (the Thirteenth, Fourteenth, and Fifteenth amendments) and women (who were granted suffrage through the Nineteenth Amendment). Second, strong antidiscrimination legislation has been enacted, as in the case of the Civil Rights Act of 1964 and the Voting Rights Act of 1965. Finally, the evolution of judicial standards has generally resulted in more liberal interpretations of citizens' rights. For example, the U.S. Supreme Court's *Brown* v. *Board of Education* decision of 1954 overturned an earlier ruling that permitted *de jure* racial segregation.[21]

The survival and even expansion of these principles of toleration throughout two centuries of increasing social and cultural diversification seems all the more remarkable in light of the recent experiences of other heterogeneous nations. Much of the international news during the 1970s, for example, was dominated by stories of minority uprisings or civil war in various parts of the world, including Lebanon, Rhodesia, Cyprus, and Northern Ireland. The question that remains, therefore, is how and why the United States has experienced comparative success and prosperity as a multiracial, multiethnic, multidenominational society. Certainly, this is an enormously complex issue and one whose resolution would take us well beyond the bounds of the present inquiry. However, one institution that, perhaps more than any other, has been given the task of promoting tolerance for human diversity is the public school. In emphasizing the contributions of public education, it will not be suggested that the preservation of racial, religious, ethnic, or political toleration within American life is exclusively a function of the schools. Yet, the case can be made that American education is especially well suited for preparing children for their roles in a highly diverse society. How the schools actually go about this task will be the subject of the following chapters.

CONCLUSION

According to law, a citizen's personal background and intellectual or political idiosyncracies are not relevant factors in his or her dealings with the state. Yet, formal guarantees of impartiality notwithstanding, Americans have historically been fascinated by social diversity and, for good and for bad, have made race, religion, ethnicity, and ideology salient considerations in both public and private endeavors. A classic illustration is the "balanced ticket," which for many years was customary in the politics of New York. Within New York City itself, each major party's slate of candidates invariably included an Irishman, an Italian, and a Jew, in recognition of the city's ethnic configuration at the time. Statewide, the formula was expanded to permit the inclusion of at least one white Anglo-Saxon Protestant candidate.

Such arrangements, and the fierce in-group loyalties that they implied, must have seemed quite bizarre to residents of the more homogeneous sections of the nation. Today, however, the "ethnic revitalization" of which we have briefly spoken has made subgroup affiliation a highly salient factor in all regions and in all institutions throughout the United States. Nowhere is this more true than in public education. In a sense, racial desegregation, multiculturalism, and mainstreaming represent the educational equivalents of the balanced ticket, in that they offer something to everybody and heighten the salience of the individual's personal background and group affiliations in the routines of daily life.

The extent to which social diversity has become a principal concern of American education is perhaps best indicated by the presence of certain highly sophisticated multicultural school programs in some very unlikely locales. Consider the case of the Charlotte-Mecklenberg (North Carolina) Public Schools. While the Charlotte area does have a sizable black population, by no stretch of the imagination could it be considered a hotbed of ethnicity. Indeed, its proportion of "foreign stock" residents (to use the census term) is among the lowest of any large city in the United States. Yet, the Charlotte-Mecklenberg schools maintain an active bilingual program, which offers instruction in no fewer than fifty-nine foreign languages, ranging from Arabic, Armenian, and Ashanti to Urdu, Vietnamese, and Yao.[22]

As this single example clearly suggests, America's public schools are expected to do more than simply respond to the increasing importance of ethnicity. They are, in fact, at the leading edge of the nation's effort to come to terms with the diversity of its people.

2

Socialization for Diversity: The Conventional Wisdom

One of the traditional concerns of educational theorists is the proper goal of public schooling within a democratic social order. Typically, the point is made that education seeks to strike a balance between the interests of individuals and the needs of society. John Dewey, for instance, identified the directive, control, and guidance functions of the school as mechanisms for accomplishing this goal. Through direction, the individual's "active tendencies . . . are led in a certain continuous course, instead of dispersing aimlessly." Guidance is "assisting through cooperation the natural tendencies of the individuals." In contrast with both of these, the control function of education relies on the application of external authority. It is the process by which the individual "is brought to subordinate his natural impulses to public or common ends."[1]

The problem of balance is greatly complicated when a democratic nation is also socially diverse. Under these circumstances, the group plays an especially important role as intermediary between the individual and the larger society. Moreover, there also exist group interests that must be considered. To some degree, individual, group, and societal interests may overlap. Thus, a person usually wants whatever is good for his or her group, and what is good for the group may also be good for the larger social system. In many instances, however, these interests are not identical, and individuals and groups may be asked to sacrifice for the greater good. Certain examples, such as taxation and military service, come readily to mind. Other, less obvious cases are discussed throughout this book, such as the demands made on subcultural minorities to abandon their familiar languages and customs in favor of those of the majority of Americans.

In a modern democracy, it is usually the public school that takes primary responsibility for reconciling these three sets of interests. *Socialization* is the term that is used to describe the process by which this balance is struck. More familiarly, socialization refers to the transmission of culture to each new generation. *Culture*, in turn, is defined as the values, attitudes, beliefs, and behaviors that are characteristic of a society or of any group. Individuals, therefore, are taught to be members both of groups and of society at large. While minor differences are not usually regarded as problematic, the culture of a group (i.e., a subculture) is expected to conform to that of the larger system. When it does not, society, in order to ensure its own survival, attempts to replace or supplement the distinctive subculture with its own pattern. Some of the ways in which modern societies have sought to achieve this goal were described in chapter 1.

Within the United States, socialization has come to be a division of labor, in which the inculcation of subcultural patterns has remained more or less the province of the family, the church, and certain voluntary organizations, while schools have focused on the transmission of the broader common culture. Of course, there are few clear boundaries to distinguish between these areas, and some critics have interpreted sex education, "values clarification," and other curricular innovations as intrusions by the school into the realm of the family. Similarly, many public school people firmly oppose the current efforts to reintroduce religious observances into the schools (see chapter 7) on the grounds that religion falls well outside the school's legitimate sphere of interest and influence. One component of socialization that generally is acknowledged to belong primarily to the schools is the *civic culture*—those norms, values, and beliefs that pertain directly to citizenship and governance. Much of the civic culture of the United States takes the form of laws and customs that regulate relationships among the diverse elements of the American population. There are, in effect, the ground rules for social and political toleration in American life in that they specify the rights and responsibilities of government, individuals, and groups in their dealings with one another.

The school has a multifaceted task in transmitting the civic culture to each new generation of Americans. It seeks to balance rights with responsibilities and the interests of individuals with those of the group and society. It also aims at both cognitive and affective outcomes, insofar as it tries to promote knowledge and understanding of, as well as loyalty to, the American system of governance. In this chapter, our interest centers on a single component of this process: the socialization of tolerance, which may be considered to be the effort to build support for those parts of the civic culture that guarantee the rights and freedom of individuals and groups.

ORIGINS AND EXPECTATIONS

The role of education as an instrument of tolerance socialization in the United States antedates the establishment of public school systems, and, in fact, goes back to the earliest days of the Republic. Because the Founding Fathers apparently were not entirely convinced that future generations of Americans would be as dedicated to the Constitution and Bill of Rights as they themselves were, they thought some means necessary whereby citizens could be trained in the principles of democracy, and convinced of their worth. Jefferson in particular foresaw the potential value of education as an agency of de-

mocratization. Some form of advanced education, Jefferson
argued, would be required of the nation's future leaders if they
were to preserve the "sacred deposit of the rights and liberties
of their fellow citizens."[2]

The emphasis on the socialization of elites, which was inherent in the views of Jefferson and his contemporaries, began in
the middle and later parts of the nineteenth century to give way
to the belief that education was a right and responsibility of all
citizens. Thus, by the turn of the century, compulsory education laws were on the books in all but a handful of states. The
rise of public education at the time can be attributed to various
factors that attended the wholesale industrialization of the
United States, and most generally to the necessity of transform-
ing an essentially agrarian populace into one willing and able to
participate effectively in the new industrial order. Clearly,
schools were expected to impart both the technical skills and
the personal orientations that were becoming increasingly desired of Americans.[3] However, industrialization also gave rise
to a massive influx of European immigrants, which in turn
created an urgent need for agencies of social integration and
cohesiveness. Much of the initial demand for public education
hinged on the belief that schools would serve as a bridge between the newcomers and the native-born majority. Horace
Mann, for instance, promoted the cause of the common school
by arguing that the mixture of races and nationalities within the
classroom would "kindle a spirit of mutual amity and respect
which the strains and cleavages of adult life could never de-
stroy."[4] In addition, the school was expected to "Americanize"
the immigrants by teaching them the language, customs, and
ways of life followed in their new land. This process included
political socialization—the transmission of the principles and
processes of American democracy. In the view of some observers, this was an especially formidable task, not only because of
the enormous numbers of immigrants, but also because very
few of the recent arrivals had had any prior experience with
democratic governance. In a widely read article entitled "Our
Schools Have Kept Us Free," the noted historian Henry Steele
Commager argued that it was primarily the efforts of public

schools that counteracted the potential threat to democracy posed by the relatively open immigration policies of the industrial era.[5]

In our own time, perpetuation of the traditions of social and political tolerance remains among the foremost goals of schooling. This is evidenced not only in the current popularity of such school programs as multicultural education, but also in the various rulings by the U.S. Supreme Court in the areas of racial segregation, school prayer, and student rights. For example, in *Brown* v. *Board of Education*, which declared school segregation laws unconstitutional, the Court stated that "compulsory school attendance laws and the great expenditures for education demonstrate our recognition of the importance of education to our democratic society. . . . It is the very foundation of good citizenship."[6]

In tracing the evolution of the American school as a principal agency of tolerance socialization, we should also consider some of the reasons that public education, more than any other institution, has assumed this function. Much of the explanation lies in the fact that the school is the one agency that modern societies have developed for the explicit purpose of cultural transmission. Writing at the turn of the century, the French sociologist Emile Durkheim observed that as societies moved toward industrialization, their institutions became more specialized. Under conditions of increasing functional differentiation, Durkheim believed that the traditional agencies of childhood socialization, especially the family and the church, would no longer be capable of imparting an appropriate core culture to succeding generations. Instead, the school, as an institution under public control and one specifically designed for socialization, would fill the vacuum, and would perpetuate those components of the culture most valued by society at large. By inculcating the common culture (in both its traditional and its modern aspects), the public school would prevent the disintegration of the newly industrialized society "into a heap of mutually antagonistic and self-seeking individuals."[7]

It would, of course, be a great exaggeration to suggest that schools have entirely supplanted other institutions of cultural transmission. Nevertheless, the contemporary American system of public education does seem to be uniquely well structured for promoting a common culture among the diverse elements of the national population. Consider the following points:

1. Education is universal. In each of the fifty states, children between the ages of six and sixteen (or thereabout) are required to partake of formal education of some type, and the vast majority of students are enrolled in *public* schools. In light of the ever-increasing amounts of time that American youth spend in the classroom (measured in terms of both educational attainments and average daily attendance), one presidential commission concluded that of all the roles that American children and adolescents are called on to play, the role of student is by far the dominant one in their lives.[8]

2. Education is relatively standardized. Although schooling is a local and state function, and might therefore be expected to show considerable variation between districts and between states, there is in fact so much uniformity in curricula, methods, and organization that there can be said to exist "a national education system," within which pupils, teachers, texts, and tests may move more or less freely.[9] Further contributing to the standardization of American education are the dismantling of racially dualistic school systems, the "mainstreaming" of the handicapped within regular classrooms, the development of large centralized facilities in rural districts (replacing the old hometown, one-room school), and the gradual entry of Native American children into local public school from the reservation schools sponsored by the Bureau of Indian Affairs.

3. Unlike other public agencies of socialization that are expected, at least in theory, to inculcate desirable patterns of valuation and belief among participants (such as prisons and the military), the audience for education consists entirely of children and adolescents, who are characteristically more receptive to socialization efforts than are adults.

Although well suited for the purposes of mass transmission of a relatively uniform cultural base, public schools in the United States have not always been successful in this regard. Certainly, there is ample evidence that public education has not served all groups equally well, as would be indicated in the lower levels of academic achievement and educational attainment among lower-income and minority students. Moreover, it remains unclear to what extent the schools' socialization efforts have resulted in the integration of diverse subpopulations within the American mainstream. Again, the perpetuation of racial inequalities in income, housing, employment, and health care and the persistence of racial/ethnic tensions and cleavage suggest that the integration of American society is far from complete. This is not to deny, however, that public schools have made some significant contributions in the management of intergroup relations in the United States. One example that has already been discussed is the role played by public education in the "Americanization" of millions of European immigrants. While historians today offer different interpretations of the nature of the schools' effects,[10] the fact remains that it was the public school, as much as any institution, that was called on for this task.

Having traced the origins of the tolerance socialization mission of American education, we may now examine the evidence on the schools' actual performance. Although the literature on this topic is voluminous, nearly all of it is of recent vintage; hence our discussion is confined to contemporary socialization practices and outcomes. Nevertheless, the overall findings in this area of research are clear and consistent, and point to the following general conclusions:

1. Education is strongly and positively associated with nearly all of the traditional indicators of tolerance for diversity. More precisely, educational attainment (years of schooling) has been found to be closely related to both political toleration, as expressed in support for the Bill of Rights and other principles of democratic governance, and social toleration,

in the form of favorable attitudes toward racial, ethnic, and religious diversity. Although these findings do not "prove" that tolerance is directly influenced by education, the research generally shows that the correlation between school attainment and both forms of toleration remains strong and reasonably stable even when potentially confounding variables such as socioeconomic status are taken into account. Thus, education does appear to play an important and independent part in the socialization of tolerance.

2. The specific ways in which schools bring about these outcomes have not been identified. For the most part, the more obvious vehicles for political and social attitude formation, such as course work, teacher attitudes and beliefs, and educational climates, have been found to have little impact on pupils' sociopolitical orientations.

Considered together, these two conclusions suggest that education does seem to promote tolerance, but not through any recognizable mechanisms of socialization. Before examining these findings and their implications, it might be helpful to gain a broader perspective on this issue by reviewing what is generally known about the nature and origins of tolerance for diversity.

THE FOUNDATIONS OF TOLERANCE

As used within the social scientific literature, the concept of tolerance (or toleration) generally describes nonhostile reactions to significant variation among human groups. Within the American research tradition, studies on this issue have most often focused on political toleration (the willingness to allow diverse or dissident world views and ideologies) and racial/ethnic relations (attitudes toward out-groups), although a smaller body of research also exists on religious and certain other forms of toleration.[11]

Explanations for the origins of tolerance and intolerance vary along a number of dimensions. While some efforts have been made to advance a sociobiological analysis of intergroup relations (see chapter 1), the more traditional interpretations have centered on individual psychology and on sociocultural factors. Psychologically oriented approaches to intolerance typically stress the effects of individual experience, particularly during childhood, on the formation of personality and ideology. The most influential of these explanations is probably that advanced by T. W. Adorno and his associates in *The Authoritarian Personality*, which attributed the incidence of prejudice and authoritarianism among adults to their exposure to especially harsh familial relationships during childhood. Authoritarianism in the home is believed to give rise to certain personality traits, including cynicism, status sensitivity, and cognitive rigidity, which in turn provide the basis for "a political philosophy and social outlook which has no room for anything but a desperate clinging to what appears strong and a disdainful rejection of whatever is relegated to the bottom."[12] Beyond its foundations in individual personality, intolerance is also thought to be a product of social statuses and roles. That is, people in certain positions come to develop racist or authoritarian tendencies, regardless of their initial psychological traits. Perhaps the best-known example of this approach is the thesis of *working-class authoritarianism*, which contends that intolerance for diversity is largely a consequence of economic and/or cultural marginality. In one variant of this argument, subgroups within the working class are seen to be in constant competition with each other, and with groups from the lowest social strata, for jobs, housing, and status. In order to protect their own immediate interests, subgroups are sometimes willing to support extremist social and political movements.[13] A related interpretation emphasizes the cultural origins of working-class authoritarianism, in that workers and their families tend to be "more isolated, less informed, less educated, [and] culturally less oriented to the abstract."[14] From this perspective, intolerance arises from ignorance and inexperience rather than from perceived group interest. Finally, some observers have argued that prejudice, discrimination, and authoritarianism are influenced by the society at large. Thus, an individual's or a group's tendencies toward intolerance are either encouraged or suppressed by a society's structure and culture. Van den Berghe, for instance, contrasts the patterns of race relations found under plantation economies (such as the old South) with those of modern industrial nations (the present-day United States).[15] In addition to economic factors, the demographic structure of a society—the relative size of subgroups, their residential patterns, and their degree of cultural uniformity—will also help to determine intergroup harmony or discord.

To summarize, it has been suggested that the general properties of tolerance or intolerance for diversity are shaped by individual personality and experience, by social statuses and roles, by the broader social environment, and perhaps by human nature itself. It should also be noted that specific manifestations of intolerance—its strength, form, and the objects to which it is directed—may also be influenced by all of the above elements. So, while intolerance is sometimes thought of as a uniformly unfavorable disposition to any significant expression of diversity, racism (or ethnocentrism) and political authoritarianism are by no means always closely connected. At the individual level, many politically liberal American whites are said to practice a subtle but consistent "aversive racism,"[16] in which contacts with blacks are generally avoided, while entire societies (the so-called herrenvolk democracies) have managed to maintain contradictory policies of racism and political democracy.[17]

In view of its enormously complex and varied origins, it might seem doubtful that tolerance for diversity among individual citizens can be substantially influenced by any single institution. Yet, as we have already seen, there is a long-standing belief among Americans that the public school is somehow able to shape the members of each new generation into the kinds of citizens who will perpetuate the ideal and reality of democratic governance and work toward a more equitable and tolerant social order. Moreover, this public belief in the democratizing influence of education appears to be remarkably strong and stable, perhaps unrealistically so. For example, although the educational attainments of the American people have increased steadily (and now average 12.5 years of schooling[18]), intolerance has not entirely disappeared. Indeed, there are signs that some forms of racism and political extremism are once again on the rise (see chapter 7). Nevertheless, the faith in education endures. A review of the research on this subject will demonstrate how well justified that faith is.

Contemporary research on social and political toleration has been greatly influenced by a handful of studies that appeared shortly after World War II. In both Europe and the United States, revelation of the full extent of the Nazi horror sparked a vastly expanded effort to understand the causes of extremism. One principal European contribution to the literature was *The Authoritarian Personality*, a series of psychologically oriented studies of the roots of intolerance that has already been discussed in this chapter. The writings of Gunnar Myrdahl, Robin M. Williams, and Gordon Allport focused particularly on the emerging crisis in American race relations.[19] Events in subsequent years, including the Supreme Court's desegregation decision in *Brown* v. *Board of Education* and the mounting fear of domestic communism, further enhanced the salience of civil rights and civil liberties as issues for research. Accordingly, it was at about this time that researchers began in-depth surveys on these questions among the American public. One of the most important of these was Samuel Stouffer's *Communism, Conformity, and Civil Liberties.*[20] Published in 1955, Stouffer's study was among the first to offer empirical documentation for the traditional belief in the democratizing influence of education. Specifically, Stouffer found that better-educated subjects were consistently more tolerant in their attitudes toward certain political questions of the day, including the citizenship rights of Communists and other nonconformists. In the years since, Stouffer's findings have been replicated in one form or another in most of the major American studies of civil libertarianism.[21] Likewise, the abundant literature on intergroup relations has shown quite clearly that educational attainment is strongly associated with lower levels of prejudice toward racial, religious, and ethnic out-groups.[22]

One potential source of ambiguity in all of these studies is the close interrelationship of education with various other background characteristics. Because educational attainment tends to be associated with other status traits (such as income and occupation), the heightened tolerance for diversity found among well-educated respondents might be more a function of these other factors than of education per se. While this point cannot be entirely discounted, it is perhaps more important that recent studies analyzing the linkage between educational attainment and tolerance have found it to be essentially independent of the influence of other background and status variables. On the whole, better-educated citizens express more tolerant attitudes than do their less-educated counterparts at nearly every level of income, occupation, community leadership, and age, and in every region of the country.[23]

All of this evidence would seem to represent solid support for the conventional wisdom that formal education promotes greater tolerance for diversity. Less clear, however, are the dynamics of this relationship. After nearly thirty years of research on the role of the school in the socialization of tolerance, very few, if any, specific policies, programs, or practices have been found to be consistently and significantly associated with students' attitudes toward social or political diversity. Because this conclusion may come as something of a surprise to some readers, and because it apparently contradicts certain fundamental assumptions about citizenship education in American schools, it will be worth our while to review the evidence on which it is based.

Political Socialization

Probably the most common assumption about civic training in the schools is that children learn the roles and responsibilities of citizenship in approximately the same way that they learn to read and write or add and subtract, that is, through direct instruction. This assumption underlies most of the more explicit mechanisms of political socialization within the school, including patriotic celebrations (skits, assemblies, and projects for national holidays), rituals (recitation of the Pledge of Allegiance), and, most important, the civics or social studies curriculum. Over the years, this assumption has been set forth in countless goal statements and policy reviews. Consider, for example, one especially influential statement issued by the Commission on the Reorganization of Secondary Education and published by the federal government's Bureau of Education in 1918. In its report, the commission argued that "good citizenship" (defined partly in terms of democratic attitudes and beliefs) should be a goal of all classroom instruction and the dominant objective of social studies course work.[24] Today, some form of civics instruction is required at most grade levels and is thought by the public at large to be among the most important of all subject areas.[25]

Apparently because the beneficial effects of social studies instruction were taken to be obvious, systematic research on this issue did not begin in earnest until the 1960s. However, several studies that appeared at that time are notable for the basic questions they raised about political socialization practices in the school. In his research on civics courses in three high schools, Litt found that subject content varied with the socioeconomic status of each school's student body.[26] Specifically, the most affluent school offered an activist, participatory interpretation of the citizen's role that was in sharp contrast with the more ritualistic emphasis of a nearby working-class high school. However, exposure to civics curricula in all three communities was associated with lower levels of political chauvinism and greater support for democratic principles. Despite this promising lead, other researchers have generally not been able to provide evidence that social studies courses exercise any decisive impact on students' political toleration. The stream of negative findings began in 1968 with the publication of an article by Langton and Jennings, which concluded that high school civics curricula had little bearing on pupils' attitudes toward civil liberties, with the exception of a positive effect on a subsample of minority students.[27] When the authors reanalyzed their data with more powerful statistical techniques, the basic findings emerged even more forcefully. It was concluded that civics courses are likely to be effective mainly in the political socialization of students who have had little prior exposure to the subject matter.[28]

Partly as a result of these studies, subsequent research has looked more closely at conditioning factors within the classroom. Several observers have suggested that the overall ineffectiveness of the typical civics curriculum as a socialization mechanism is due to the blandness of its content. In particular, few high school social studies courses delve into sensitive and controversial topics such as civil liberties.[29] Thus, it has been proposed that curricula that directly address such issues will have significant impact on students' political tolerance. And, indeed, some of the findings on this question offer encouragement. Several studies of short courses in civil liberties have reported positive effects, although these gains have been relatively modest and conditional.[30] Another factor that has received consideration is the intellectual and interpersonal tone of the classroom. Ehman found that discussion of controversial issues backfired unless conducted in an atmosphere of open inquiry,[31] and Goldenson discovered that gains in civil libertarianism varied with the perceived credibility of the instructor.[32] More generally, Ehman has concluded that the open classroom tends to facilitate formation of democratic attitudes.[33] However, the most systematic investigations of the political effects of classroom climates are contained in several cross-cultural studies of civics education in the United States and Europe. Using large samples and advanced research designs, researchers discovered that classroom settings and teacher characteristics account for little of the variation in pupils' adherence to democratic principles.[34] Similarly, a negative view of teachers' influence emerges from the research of

Jennings, Ehman, and Niemi, who conclude that teachers operate at "the margins rather than at the vitals of adolescent political toleration."[35]

If various classroom factors appear to have no consistent effect on students' attitudes toward diversity, it may be partly because pupils are differentially disposed to receive the messages transmitted to them. Dawson and Prewitt suggest that students are more likely to absorb the normative content of civics instruction when course content does not conflict with the political orientations of the home, peer group, and community.[36] Political learning is also likely to be tied to intellectual ability. It is generally presumed that a clear understanding of political principles and ideologies requires a relatively advanced level of cognitive development.[37] The available evidence supports this view: Appreciation of democratic ideals, including the rights of individual citizens, has been found to be positively related to overall academic ability and to civics knowledge.[38] However, in most of these studies, the observed effects of cognitive variables on measures of political toleration were rather modest. (The exception is Neilsen's research, which showed that the influence of civics knowledge on toleration of dissent was substantially stronger than that of any other variable or set of variables.[39])

In summary, the conventional wisdom about the methods of tolerance socialization—that it is directly taught to students in regular civics courses—is generally not substantiated by research findings. Whatever prospect exists for teaching political tolerance would seem to center on experimental programs that utilize an open-classroom format in addressing the issues of civil rights and liberties.

In recent years, researchers have gone beyond curricular and instructional factors in hopes of explaining the relationship between education and political tolerance. Two broad sets of variables that have received the greatest attention are students' participation in the social network of their schools and the overall governance climate of schools and program tracks. With respect to the former, it is well known that adolescent peer groups exercise wide-ranging influence on students' academic values, aspirations, and achievements.[40] However, it is uncertain how far this influence extends into the area of political toleration. Some cross-cultural research indicates that certain peer-group activities, such as democratic decision-making and political discussion, have a positive but very limited effect on the attitudes of both European and American secondary school pupils.[41] Similar results of peer socialization are reported by Langton in a study of Jamaican schools.[42] In this case, greater support for democratic values was found among middle-class children and those working-class youngsters who were friendly with middle-class schoolmates, leading to the conclusion that the latter group exercised a democratizing influence. However, it seems equally plausible that these working-class pupils may have sought friendships among schoolmates whom they perceived to share their own values, including, perhaps, political orientations. This interpretation is supported by the conclusion of Levin that peer socialization is most effective among youngsters with a strong interest in politics.[43] In these cases, peer groups appear to provide opportunities for open, bilateral exchange of ideas that may be less forthcoming in contacts with adults. Another aspect of the school's social network that is sometimes seen as contributing to political socialization is extracurricular activities. According to its proponents, the high school activity program affords pupils the chance for leadership, cooperation, and responsibility—the very stuff of which democratic citizenship is said to be made. In addition, it is believed to provide participants with firsthand experience in applying democratic procedures of rule making and conflict resolution.[44] Nevertheless, despite whatever effects school activities may have on other political attitudes, they have been found to have little if any direct impact on students' orientations toward civil liberties.[45] Research has also considered the possible influence of schools' governance policies on students' attitude formation. In brief, the hypothesis here is that both school climates and the attitudes they induce vary along socioeconomic lines. According to Bowles and Gintis, and others, the rigid, authoritarian policies to which working-class pupils are exposed result in a heightened sense of alienation and a greater willingness to accept authoritarianism as a normal part of social life.[46] Once again, however, the evidence does not consistently support this proposition. While greater alienation has been found among pupils in an authoritarian school[47] and among working-class high school students in a noncollege track,[48] results of other studies suggest that schoolwide governance climates and structures have a mixed or limited effect on students' attitudes.[49]

The appropriate conclusion therefore seems to be that researchers have so far been largely unsuccessful in their attempts to identify instructional, climatic, or organizational properties of the public school that show a clear, consistent relationship with the formation of politically tolerant attitudes. Those factors that appear to have a potentially stronger influence, such as the politically aware peer group or the social studies class that allows a "no holds barred" approach to controversial issues, are probably best regarded as exceptions to ordinary school experiences, and thus not a major factor in the socialization of most students.

Racial Relations

In addition to fostering support for political democracy, the American public school is expected to serve as a proving ground for social integration and intergroup toleration. The rationale here has several aspects. Over the long run, education exposes diverse groups to a shared system of values, beliefs, and knowledge, which, having been internalized during the school years, will allow adults of varying backgrounds to coexist in relative harmony and to work cooperatively for the attainment of the general social welfare. Schools are also expected to produce immediate payoffs in the form of heightened tolerance among students. Children, it is argued, are receptive to socialization efforts. They can, in particular, be directly taught positive attitudes and beliefs about human diversity. At the same time, the socially diverse nature of their enrollments will allow many schools to serve as "a natural laboratory" for human relations.[50] Since children tend to be less prejudiced than their elders, most of their intergroup contacts are likely to be of a positive nature and thereby provide healthy experience in cross-racial and cross-ethnic situations. It is precisely this type of experience that Cohen appears to have had in mind when she suggested that students in desegregated schools "are being asked to solve the problems of integration which their parents have been unable to handle in society at large."[51]

The record of the schools' actual performance in fostering mutual acceptance among groups is somewhat ambiguous. As has already been mentioned, little hard evidence is available on public education's effects on religious or ethnic toleration among whites. There is, however, a substantial literature on the school's service as an agency of racial toleration. Most of the available research on this topic falls into two categories: evaluations of instructional programs intended to change racial attitudes, and studies of the effects of school desegregation. Important differences exist between these two approaches. While nearly all of the latter research has been conducted in the last twenty-five years, many of the evaluations of race-relations training courses were undertaken in the years prior to the wholesale desegregation of American education. In addition, the earlier work often utilized experimental frameworks, while desegregation research tends toward cross-sectional, survey designs. Despite differences in design and method, both lines of research converge on one major conclusion—that specific school experiences have only a modest bearing on students' racial attitudes.

INSTRUCTIONAL APPROACHES.　According to Katz, the original public school courses in race relations consisted of a "frontal assault" on prejudice and were based on the belief that racism and ethnocentrism are functions of ignorance, which can best be counteracted by providing positive information about out-groups.[52] Over the years, the frontal assault, at least in its original form, has gradually been abandoned by the schools, although it remains in use in other institutions, including the military. As has been noted in several reviews, a purely instructional approach proved to be ineffective in changing students' attitudes. Somewhat more successful were experimental programs that included a strong affective component, such as those involving simulation and role playing, and those in which pupils were able to identify with instructors perceived as holding positive racial attitudes and beliefs.[53] However, with the implementation of desegregation, many educators apparently felt that lectures or course work in race relations would be superfluous or even counterproductive: If pupils were getting along reasonably well, there would be no need for instruction in this matter; conversely, if tensions did exist, they might be exacerbated by courses that only emphasized intergroup differences.

The demise of frontal-assault techniques does not necessarily mean that public schools have excluded subcultural concerns from their curricula. On the contrary, by the mid-1970s, no fewer than twenty states required some form of multicultural education. The updated version of racial/ethnic instruction, however, tends to be much more broad-ranging than the old courses and is aimed as much at minority-group pupils as at whites. Multicultural education is discussed in chapter 6. For now, suffice it to say that very little research or evaluational data on the new courses have been reported.

SCHOOL DESEGREGATION.   If the effectiveness of direct instruction in the formation of racial tolerance remains a relatively underexplored area of educational research, the same cannot be said of the study of intergroup relations in desegregated schools. In brief, the prevailing assumption here has been that by being placed in the same schools and classrooms, students of varied backgrounds will gradually come to accept each other and develop favorable racial attitudes. In large part, the origins of this approach can be traced to the "contact" theory of intergroup relations. As originally developed by Robin M.

Williams, Gordon Allport, and others, contact theory maintains that conditions of status equality, cooperative effort toward common goals, and strong institutional support will promote a reasonable degree of mutual acceptance and understanding between groups, which in turn will lead to a willingness to engage in further contacts.[54] Yet most desegregation researchers have made only very limited attempts to apply contact theory in its entirety to the case of the racially desegregated school. Instead, studies have tended to explore the relationship between one or two indicators of desgregation (often the racial balance of the school or classroom) and students' levels of racial prejudice. By now, this literature has been systematically examined in a number of reviews, which have uniformly concluded that school desegregation in and of itself has no clear and consistent impact on children's racial attitudes.[55] Nor do specific properties of the desegregation plan (e.g., mandatory vs. voluntary) or of the research design itself (longitudinal as opposed to cross-sectional) seem to be associated with the strength or direction of reported attitude change.[56] However, most reviewers have been strongly critical of various practices within this line of research, including its incomplete application of contact theory and its overreliance on standard attitudinal measures of racial tolerance.

Perhaps as a consequence of these criticisms, desegregation studies published in recent years have begun to move away from the familiar survey/questionnaire approach, and have adopted a broader range of methodologies, including experimentation, ethnography, and systematic observation of classroom interaction. In contrast with the findings of most attitudinal studies of desegregation, the recent evidence suggests that students' intergroup relations, measured in terms of the frequency and purpose of cross-racial interactions, are often significantly affected by school and classroom variables. What appears to be important here are the climate and structure found within the classroom, including the degree of interpersonal warmth projected by the teacher, the even-handed treatment of racial groups, and the availability of diverse instructional arrangements, especially cooperative work groups.[57] The central role of the teacher is also suggested by a variety of findings that positive contacts diminish in unsupervised or voluntary activities. For example, lunchrooom seating and extracurricular participation often show a high degree of within-group clustering, and unsupervised classrooom work groups are sometimes marked by interracial tension and misunderstanding.[58]

Based on the findings reported in both major lines of research on students' intergroup relations, the most appropriate conclusion appears to be that racial attitudes are relatively impervious to manipulation by educators, whether through direct instruction or provision of contact opportunities. On the other hand, when the focus is shifted from attitudes to children's interaction patterns, teachers' instructional and management behaviors become a key determinant of relationships among white and minority pupils.

THE INFLUENCE OF COLLEGES AND UNIVERSITIES

So far, our discussion has focused entirely on socialization mechanisms in elementary and secondary schools. Yet some observers believe that it is not until students reach the college or university that they adopt more tolerant racial and political attitudes. According to Dye and Zeigler, the content of civics instruction and the intellectual climate of the schools are such as to promote a simplified, uncritical view of social and political life, which "does not necessarily include respect for the rights of minorities."[59] In this argument, college and university life is thought to be qualitatively different from the lower levels of schooling, especially as it is marked by an atmosphere of free inquiry that leads students to reexamine their previous beliefs.

Much of the available evidence seems to lend support to this argument. One retrospective study, for instance, found that young people attending college were less authoritarian than an initially similar sample of their high school classmates whose education ended with twelfth grade.[60] Similarly, Feldman and Newcomb discovered levels of prejudice, dogmatism, and authoritarianism to be consistently higher among freshmen than among seniors at several institutions.[61] While these studies do not rule out the possibility of selection (i.e., the initially less tolerant do not attend college, or drop out before graduation), the fact that controls were imposed on most background characteristics appears to support the conclusion that higher education often does lead to more flexible attitudes toward diversity. However, if the college experience were preeminently important in the development of tolerance, as Dye and Zeigler have claimed, we would expect the gains associated with each additional year of higher education to be of greater magnitude than those associated with every additional year of elementary or secondary schooling. And on this point, the argument falls short. A wide range of evidence indicates that the relationship between tolerance and education is essentially linear, increasing steadily with each increment in attainment.[62] Probably the most extensive analysis of this issue can be found in the recent work of Hyman and Wright.[63] In examining response patterns on a wide range of sociopolitical items, the authors found many questions on which college education was associated with a sharper increase in civil libertarianism than were other levels of schooling. There are also, however, numerous cases in which precisely the opposite was true. Overall, the pattern in Hyman and Wright's work, and in most of the other research, is one of steady gains. Hence, the college or university appears to be no more important in the socialization of tolerance than are the other levels of education.

ATTITUDES AS EDUCATIONAL PRIORITIES

In certain respects, the finding that students' social and political attitudes are so little affected by either formal or informal socialization activities within the school is not surprising. Despite the substantial lipservice paid to the affective domain, it seems fair to suggest that the major preoccupation of the school's formal organization is academic instruction. The rewards most important to students (such as grades, letters of recommendation, and the diploma itself) depend far more on students' ability to master subject matter than on their professed allegiance to the principles of democracy. Thus, students are regularly tested on what they know, but are seldom asked how they feel about a social or political issue. If they are asked (usually in a survey or questionnaire), they are told that their responses "don't count" toward a grade. Much the same point applies to the informal organization of the schools. As we have seen in this chapter, numerous social and interpersonal factors within the school environment have been hypothesized as potential determinants of students' attitudes toward diversity. Yet rarely have these expectations been supported by results. One likely explanation for this is that the schools' climates and informal structures exist primarily for reasons other than the transmission of sociopolitical principles. A particularly vivid example is the high school extracurricular activity. In theory, as mentioned earlier, schools maintain activity programs partly to facilitate democratic socialization. In practice, however, extracurricular activities serve a variety of other functions. Some of these are obvious: Varsity sports can help to unify a school and even a community; clubs and hobby groups teach skills; and all or nearly all activities are expected to enhance the students' sense of belonging or engagement within the school. In addition, some observers have called attention to the subtler benefits of the extracurriculum as a mechanism for ensuring students' compliance with rules and regulations in both the high school and in later life.[64]

The point is that within public education the affective components of the civic culture—specifically the values, beliefs, and attitudes that underlie political and social toleration—are typically approached as abstract, long-range goals rather than as concrete objectives for which students (or, for that matter, teachers and principals) are held accountable. And even when schools have deliberately attempted to influence students' attitudes, they have relied most heavily on relatively simplistic methods (such as traditional teacher-centered instruction and manipulation of racial balance in enrollments) that have rarely been productive.

None of this should be taken to suggest that public schools are necessarily ineffective in building support for the principles of civic and social tolerance. On the contrary, instances were cited throughout the preceding research review in which results were clearly positive. Common to most successful approaches, not surprisingly, is an emphasis on the affective domain, and particularly the provision of situations in which students become directly engaged in discussions or applications of the principles of toleration. These include cooperative interracial work groups, simulation and role playing, appropriate role modeling by teachers, and open-classroom discussions of current controversies. Another promising approach along these lines, which has not yet been systematically evaluated, is multicultural education. In some of its varieties, multiculturalism places strong emphasis on affective outcomes, including the development of mutual understanding and acceptance among students of diverse racial and ethnic origins.

Thus, for educators who are genuinely interested in changing students' racial or political attitudes, research has provided at least a handful of clues as to the appropriate courses of action. Realistically, however, these programs can be expected to remain in much the same status as they are now—exceptions to the normal course of events within the school. Such efforts may simply require too large an investment of teachers' time and energy, or be too provocative to win the approval of principals, superintendents, and school boards. There is, moreover, the larger question of whether most educators actually intend, expect, or hope to influence the social and political attitudes of their students. As has already been suggested, cognitive matters typically have priority over affective outcomes, if not in a school district's formal goal statements, then at least in its day-to-day operations. However, there is another type of socialization outcome to which attitudes, values, and beliefs are usually subordinate, and that is the individual's actual behavior. If teachers and administrators were asked to rank tolerant attitudes and tolerant behaviors as educational priorities, we might very well expect them to choose the latter. As a practical matter, a friendly, orderly environment within a racially diverse school is usually preferable to one in which students' tolerance for diversity is confined to the realm of abstract political or social ideals. Of course, schools might, and often do, try to promote both types of outcome, but as the research has begun to show, they tend to be more effective in influencing students' actual behaviors. In fact, public schools in the United States have been highly successful in this regard, as I will demonstrate in the following chapter.

CONCLUSION

Thirty or so years of sustained research into the relationship between formal education and individuals' tolerance for diversity has produced only partial support for the conventional wisdom on this issue. As expected, exposure to education is clearly and closely associated with support for democratic political principles and with relatively favorable attitudes toward racial and other out-groups. Contrary to the prevailing assumptions, formation of these attitudes is not appreciably influenced by any specific educational experiences.

That American education appears to be reasonably successful in fostering tolerance for diversity is reassuring. That it does so by means unknown and unexplained is not. In the absence of any clear understanding of the dynamics of tolerance socialization, little firm basis exists for formulating future policies, or even for evaluating those that already exist. Thus, there is an obvious need to unravel the mystery currently surrounding this issue.

3

Education and Tolerance: A Reappraisal

In *The Structure of Scientific Revolutions*, Thomas Kuhn argues that the growth of human knowledge has been restricted by intellectual fashions, and especially by the tendency of scientific disciplines to rely on a single paradigm, or mode of inquiry. The power of a dominant paradigm may be such as to effectively foreclose the pursuit of knowledge through alternative approaches, thereby limiting the types of questions that are asked, and the answers that are accepted. When this happens, research and theorizing arrive at an impasse, which is resolved only with the emergence of a new paradigm.[1]

The field of tolerance research now appears to be at such an impasse. With the general conclusion that tolerance for diversity is a function more of the amount of schooling that individuals receive than of the ways in which they are educated, this line of inquiry has ceased to be a source of useful insight for educational policymakers. Consider, for example, an interpretation advanced in one major study. According to Nunn, Crockett, and Williams, tolerance is a by-product of one's cumulative educational history. Education is seen as an inherently broadening process that exposes the individual to new ideas, new experiences, and new ways of seeing things. The more familiar students become with social and intellectual diversity, the less threatened they will be. Hence, support for civil rights and civil liberties gradually emerges from the overall process of education, and it is this "cultural sophistication" or "cosmopolitanism" that explains the very strong correlation between educational attainment and tolerance for diversity.[2]

This interpretation has considerable appeal in that it reconciles two apparently contradictory findings—the strong effects of education in general and the weak effects of specific school experiences—while also holding out the comforting prospect that problems of intolerance in the United States will eventually be resolved by the ever-increasing educational attainment of the American people. However, it is also badly flawed in some respects. In particular, this argument and the research on which it is based posit a very narrow conception of tolerance for diversity, one that is no longer widely accepted in other branches of social science. It suggests that tolerance is meaningfully reflected in the attitudes of individuals toward abstract ideals or hypothetical situations, while the conviction has been growing elsewhere that the most important displays of tolerance for diversity are those that occur in the course of citizens' actual behavior. In addition, there are long-standing technical problems in measuring racial and political attitudes that cast doubt on the validity of this type of inquiry.

This chapter will explore the conceptual and methodological shortcomings of traditional research, and present the case for behaviorally centered studies. In so doing, it also shows that public schools are more effective in promoting tolerant behavior than is currently recognized.

THE LIMITATIONS OF TOLERANCE RESEARCH

Tolerance for diversity is widely acknowledged to be a highly complex, multidimensional concept. According to Ferrar, social or political toleration should be assessed not only by measuring the strength and direction of sentiments and their association with other aspects of personality, but also by determining the extent to which subjects are willing to take appropriate action in support of those sentiments.[3] In other words, tolerance has both attitudinal and behavioral components. Nevertheless, the vast majority of studies on this issue have employed only attitudinal indicators of tolerance. Research on racial/ethnic relations has characteristically used surveys and questionnaires to measure prejudice toward out-groups, while the literature on political authoritarianism has focused on subjects' responses to abstract or hypothetical statements concerning civil liberties. Rarely has the behavioral dimension of racial or political toleration received similar attention.

The strong emphasis on attitudinal research that pervades this field can be attributed to several factors. First, there is the influence of structural functionalism, which has been described as the dominant paradigm of contemporary social science.[4] Structuralist interpretations generally stress the importance of values as determinants of social phenomena. For tolerance researchers working within this tradition, racial and political values are thought to be manifested in attitudes. Second, as a practical matter, attitudinal measures are convenient to administer. As was noted some half-century ago by LaPiere, questionnaires are "cheap, easy, and mechanical," whereas behavioral observation is "time consuming [and] fatiguing."[5] Third, there are some circumstances in which other forms of inquiry are simply not possible. St. John, for instance, argues that in studying the effects of desegregation on race relations, some form of pre/post measure is required. Since intergroup contacts do not occur in any meaningful sense in a segregated institution, attempts to compare interaction patterns before and after desegregation would be much less productive than comparisons of attitude change.[6]

Despite these advantages, attitudinal approaches to tolerance research pose several major problems for social scientists.

Although attitudes are said to be no less real than overt actions,[7] most observers would probably agree with Deutscher's assertion that the ultimate goal of social science is to explain and predict human *behavior*.[8] That is, we tend to be more interested in what people actually do in a given circumstance than in what they say they will do. Theoretically, of course, attitudes and behaviors are closely related. Indeed, attitudes are generally defined as sets of beliefs that dispose one to act in a preferential manner.[9] However, research indicates that a person's attitudes often have little bearing on behavior. The difficulty is not so much that the attitude-action correlation is uniformly weak, but rather that it is highly variable and that many of the conditions under which it is strengthened or weakened remain poorly understood.[10] Generally, it is presumed that an individual's behavior is subject to a wide range of influences, including normative and situational constraints, one's own social and intellectual abilities, competing motivations, and the interests of other participants.[11] Stated simply, it is often difficult, and sometimes impossible, for people to act solely on the basis of their own attitudes. Related to this is the problem of capturing what subjects actually think or feel about an issue. Once again, there are numerous instances in which a subject's verbal or written response to a survey item is generated by something other than his or her feelings about the matter at hand. Of considerable importance here is the survey or interview situation itself. Especially on sensitive or controversial issues, such as civil liberties or racial relations, participants may be tempted to provide socially desirable responses whether or not those responses reflect their own underlying beliefs or attitudes. Respondents might be embarrassed about their feelings, or reluctant to "go on record" with them.[12] Thus, studies have found wide disparities not only between attitudes and behaviors pertaining to tolerance, but also between attitudes toward different formulations of the principle of racial or political toleration.[13] To reiterate, the method by which data on tolerance are gathered may be an important determinant of findings.

This problem has important implications for understanding

the role of education in fostering tolerance for diversity. In view of the simplistic, transparent survey items often employed in this line of research,[14] it is highly probable that many respondents will "see through" the purpose of a question and adjust their answers accordingly. Indications are that this pattern of response acquiescence is especially evident among better-educated subjects, who understand how their responses will be interpreted and, thus forewarned, may choose to provide a disguise for any intolerant views they hold.[15] When practiced on a large scale, the net result is an inflated estimate of the correlation between educational attainment and the advocacy of racial and political toleration.

An additional problem with tolerance surveys occurs in research on children's attitudes. When surveys are administered in a classroom setting (as they often are), students may perceive the questionnaire as a test (even if they are assured otherwise), and attempt to provide a "correct" answer rather than one that reflects their own beliefs. When an item is especially transparent, nearly all subjects may choose the same response, which would prevent the emergence of a significant correlation between students' attitudes and the educational stimulus (a textbook, course, or climate) that is being evaluated. For the most part, this pattern can be expected to occur among older students, especially those in senior high schools. Among younger students, the problem is different but the result the same—a weakened correlation between educational input and attitudinal response. As Renshon has pointed out, there is a tendency among researchers to assume that survey items dealing with sociopolitical issues have the same significance for children that they have for adults.[16] This assumption, however, flies in the face of a considerable body of evidence showing that an accurate grasp of democratic principles is possible only at a relatively advanced stage of cognitive development, usually early to mid-adolescence.[17] So, when elementary-grade students are presented with a survey on race relations or civil liberties, they are being asked about matters to which they have given no previous thought and of which they may have little understanding. The responses provided, then, can hardly be taken as evidence of deeply felt, personal sentiments. Nor are they useful indicators of the effects of a particular educational experience. Davidson makes much the same point in suggesting that attitudinal surveys typically overlook the "human context" of children's intergroup relations. The child who, for whatever reason, provides ethnocentric responses to a questionnaire can very often be found happily engaged in a racially mixed play group shortly after the questionnaire has been administered.[18]

To summarize, it has been argued that prevailing research practices have resulted in an overestimate of the correlation between tolerance and educational attainment, and an underestimate of the influence of specific school experiences. This conclusion casts doubt on the claim, reviewed in this chapter, that tolerance for diversity is a cumulative by-product of the overall educational process. It also suggests, in more general terms, that socialization practices within the school may be more effective in transmitting politically and racially tolerant attitudes than would seem to be indicated by the existing research.

However, there is an even more fundamental issue posed by the attitudinal-centered approach to tolerance research—namely, that individuals' verbal or written attitudes toward civil liberties or racial relations are simply not very useful or meaningful indicators of toleration. Instead, there is a growing conviction among sociologists and political scientists that in a complex, heterogeneous nation, the true measure of citizens' tolerance for diversity lies in their willingness to accept those individual and group differences that are encountered in the course of ordinary social interactions. From this perspective, what one feels or thinks or believes about intergroup relations or political dissent is of far less consequence than what one does about it. Accordingly, the schools may be seen as promoting tolerance for diversity as they inculcate the norms, dispositions, and capacities for tolerant behavior in real-life situations. The development of this interpretation and its implications for the study of tolerance socialization in the public schools are evidenced in the evolution of the idea of tolerance.

Changing Conceptions of Tolerance

Over the years, popular consensus on basic values has been said to be the glue that keeps American society intact. Tocqueville, for instance, stated that for a democratic nation to survive and to prosper, "it is necessary that the minds of all citizens should be rallied and held together by certain predominant ideas."[19] Among contemporary writers, consensus has usually been interpreted as a very high level of agreement within the public at large on the basic principles of democracy, including freedom of thought, freedom of speech, and equality of justice and opportunity. Thus, political scientists have argued that broad support for the operations of democratic government is essential to the continued stability of the political system,[20] while sociologists have stressed the need for a shared core of values among diverse elements of a population as a basis for the integration of a society.[21]

In recent years, these assumptions have been called into question. More precisely, the nature or degree of consensus that is required for the endurance of a politically democratic and socially diverse nation is now thought to be somewhat different from that suggested in traditional theory. Studies of American political opinion have concluded that the general public's support for democratic principles tends to be shallow and superficial and that genuine understanding and appreciation of these values is not widespread. Particularly striking is the finding that when civil libertarian ideals are formulated in concrete terms and applied to specific cases, levels of agreement among the public at large will usually drop sharply. For example, in one study that found that only one out of ten respondents disagreed with the abstract principle of "free speech for all," about half of the sample endorsed the statement that "a book that contains wrong political views cannot be a good book and does not deserve to be published." An even greater proportion was willing to accept the statement that "freedom of speech does not give anyone the right to teach foreign ideas in our schools."[22] Similar results have been reported elsewhere.[23] Toleration in the abstract also appears to be characteristic of the racial attitudes of many Americans. Today, few respondents are willing to acknowledge openly that they fear or dislike minority groups or to endorse obviously racist ideas. Instead, prejudice is often expressed more subtly—in code words, or in opposition to specific policies intended to promote racial integration.[24]

Partly as a response to these and related research findings, political theorists have in the past few decades moved away from the position that true democracy hinges on the active support of the public at large. While theoretical reformulations have proceeded in a variety of directions, many now seem to accept the premise that "the survival of democracy depends upon the commitment of elites to democratic ideals rather than upon broad support for democracy by the masses."[25] The accumulated evidence has consistently shown that elite groups (also described as "political influentials" or "community leaders") have a clearer understanding of, and stronger commitment to, the principles of political toleration than does the general public.[26] The linkage between the political orientations of elites and the maintenance of the democratic system has been interpreted in several ways. Proponents of the theory of democratic pluralism argue that the extremely complex nature of modern society has concentrated extensive power and authority in the hands of those experts who dominate the major institutional sectors of American life. In turn, these corporate, political, military, labor, and academic leaders vie with each other to influence government decisions, and it is precisely this diffusion of influence among contending groups that has generally prevented extreme abuses and contributed to the endurance of democracy.[27] Other writers, such as Dye and Ziegler,[28] suggest that it is the enlightened self-interest of a small, relatively homogeneous nationwide elite that is the ultimate foundation of American democracy. But in both approaches, the abstention of the mass public from serious involvement in civic affairs is seen as a "necessary condition for the creative functioning of the elite."[29] What is required of ordinary citizens is not necessarily an active commitment to democracy, but simply a willingness to go along with existing arrangements. Lipset and Raab describe this as a "loyalty . . . based on an inertia of investment in the country, system, and the traditional political structure."[30]

Somewhat the same point also applies to racial and ethnic relations. Van den Berghe has argued that value consensus provides a weak basis for social integration since it is extremely difficult to attain in a truly pluralistic society. Instead, a diverse nation is held together by "a mixture of political coercion and economic interdependence."[31] Similarly, Patterson maintains that intergroup relations is one of the very few aspects of a social system that is governed much less by shared values than by "grudgingly obeyed laws or, in the worst instance, by a selfish, Hobbesian fear of chaos and disorder."[32] This point has been amply illustrated in the changing patterns of racial relations in the United States in the years following the *Brown* v. *Board of Education* ruling. Apparently, the successful desegregation of institutions does not require participants' support for the principles of racial equality or human brotherhood. Rather, the single most important factor is very often the willingness and ability of authorities to apply enforcement mechanisms that ensure participants' compliance with the desegregation mandate. In such instances, the costs of resistance (e.g., loss of job, loss of revenue, fines, or even imprisonment) often outweigh emotional or ideological considerations. So, while implementation does not always produce changes in the values of participants, it can and frequently does create a climate of acceptance for desegregation.[33]

FUNCTIONAL TOLERANCE AND THE SCHOOLS

The implications of these developments for the study of tolerance socialization seem to be clear enough. Rather than a set of verbalized responses to abstract statements or hypothetical cases, the most meaningful manifestations of tolerance for diversity are those displayed in the course of routine social behavior. Given the high degree of interdependence that exists in a complex, pluralistic society, it is essential that groups arrive at a *modus vivendi* that recognizes the rights and interests of each opposing party, while also providing for the attainment of common goals.[34] Tolerance, therefore, should be measured by the extent to which an individual successfully participates in such arrangements.

To distinguish between the emerging and traditional conceptions of tolerance (as concrete and symbolic orientations toward diversity, respectively), we will refer to the former as "functional tolerance." Just as functional literacy describes the minimum level of language and communication skills required of citizens, so too does functional tolerance refer to certain basic social dispositions needed for successful participation in modern institutions. Functional tolerance is simply the willingness and ability to work with members of diverse groups in pursuit of individual and common goals. Moreover, it is the functional rather than symbolic variety of tolerance that appears to be the ultimate objective of racial desegregation within public education. In the words of Elizabeth Cohen:

> The mechanism of desegregation is not intended to create universal love and brotherhood. The goal of the desegregation process is a reasonable degree of social integration and a lack of overt conflict whereby blacks and whites, given an objective important to both, can trust each other and listen to each other sufficiently well to complete the task at hand.[35]

To some extent, the recently reported observational studies of desegregated classrooms represent the beginnings of a research base for understanding the development of functional tolerance among students. As was briefly discussed in chapter 2, an increasing body of evidence points consistently to certain factors within the school and classroom that foster friendly or at least neutral interactions between white and minority pupils. These include positive teacher attitudes and behaviors and the use of cooperative interracial work groups.[36] But however useful such research may be in revealing where and when desirable cross-racial contacts occur, it typically provides little evidence as to why such behaviors take place. Thus, this approach stops short of providing the full range of data needed for understanding the dynamics of tolerance socialization within the school.

To illustrate this point, it might be useful to consider briefly one study conducted at the onset of a district's desegregation program in the mid-1970s.[37] The research team (of which I was a member) was attempting to identify classroom factors that influenced various types of cross-racial interaction among elementary school students. After observing ninety-nine classes, we discovered that most types of intergroup contact occurred more frequently in classrooms where the teacher projected a feeling of warmth and acceptance, and less frequently in rooms where a "strictly business" atmosphere prevailed. On the other hand, work-related interactions were most in evidence in classes in which the teacher was especially patient and persistent in dealing with children, and which were characterized by a wide range of instructional activities. From these findings, it was surmised that the teacher plays a critical role in children's intergroup relations by setting the overall tone or climate and by structuring the contact opportunities that are available.

These findings and conclusions are fairly typical of much of the recent desegregation research. As policy guidelines, results such as these help to identify specific classroom conditions that appear to be associated with constructive cross-racial contacts. In other words, studies of this type suggest some of the things that teachers should and should not do to promote better working relationships within a socially diverse classroom. There are, however, important limitations to this approach. In particular, this line of research usually offers descriptions rather than explanations of the conditions under which functional tolerance occurs. Other than speculation, little effort is made to account for the linkages between teacher behavior or organizational structure and the frequencies and types of students' interactions.

Much of the explanation for the occurrence of successful intergroup relationships among students might be found in the normative climates of the school and classroom, particularly in the standards for pupil behavior. Recall the suggestion that racial relations in pluralist societies depend largely on the enforcement of specific rules and policies. This may be especially true in those institutions, such as the public school, where virtually *all* forms of behavior are subject to close regulation. Practically speaking, children have a much more limited range of behavioral options in the school than elsewhere. Hence, to account for the persistence or variation of a given pattern of conduct, we should look not only at the conditions under which such behavior occurs, but also at the norms underlying those conditions. An interesting illustration of this point can be found in Bossert's work on task relationships in the classroom, which revealed that certain patterns of teacher-student interaction usually thought to be functions of teacher personality traits are actually responses to the underlying norms of different teaching methods. For instance, teachers' criticism of students occurred more frequently in large-group activities, which are characterized by universalistic standards (those that apply to all participants), than in one-on-one instruction. In an individualized situation, the teacher is more likely to consider a student's own needs and abilities—in other words, to apply norms of particularism.[38]

The point is that the norms underlying school routines may have a strong, though subtle, effect on various classroom activities, including, perhaps, students' intergroup behavior. Neither teachers nor pupils need be consciously aware of these norms. Traditionally, however, the gradual internalization of these standards by students has been regarded as critical to the school's effectiveness as an agency of socialization. The process by which norms are transmitted in the classroom and their possible effects on children's acquisition of functional tolerance require detailed description.

Normative Transmission in the Classroom

In his classic treatises on the sociology of education, Emile Durkheim argued that the overriding goal of schools is to transmit the culture or morality of the larger society.[39] In particular, Durkheim saw the social objectives of schooling as threefold: discipline (regularity of conduct and acceptance of authority), autonomy (the application of reliable knowledge as a guide to behavior), and a sense of personal affiliation with groups.[40] If the child successfully acquires these orientations, he or she is equipped for full participation in society. According to Durkheim, the means by which the school achieves these outcomes is its pedagogy, or theory of education. While Durkheim's pedagogical writings include some consideration of the substantive content of school—that is, the formal curriculum—they place greater emphasis on the structural characteristics of the classroom. Hence, the most effective socialization experiences occur not as a result of formal instruction in social morality (to use Durkheim's term), but rather through the child's patterned interactions with teachers and classmates. In the course of their routine school experiences, children absorb the norms of discipline, autonomy, and affiliation that will allow them in both the present and the future "to play a personal role in the collective life."[41]

Durkheim's emphasis on the implicit social lessons of classroom experience is reflected in the writings of contemporary sociologists. According to Parsons, children's exposure to certain aspects of the classroom routine (e.g., grouping by age, systematic evaluation, and the clear demarcation of authority between teacher and pupil) allows students to develop various skills, capacities, and orientations useful for adult role performances.[42] Elaborating on this point, Dreeben has identified four norms transmitted in the ordinary course of classroom life.[43] These norms, and the means by which they are acquired, are as follows:

1. Independence, fostered primarily by the high ratio of students to teachers, which requires considerable unsupervised effort and self-reliance by pupils.
2. Achievement, acquired through classroom grading practices which stress competition against a standard of excellence.

3. Universalism, which students learn as a result of their own treatment as members of a social category (e.g., kindergarteners, third-graders), rather than as individuals.
4. Specificity (the application of limited precise criteria for evaluation), also learned through the emphasis on performance and the disregard for background characteristics.[44]

In suggesting that this socialization process is characteristic of nearly all schools, Dreeben attempts to show how formal education anticipates the structures, conditions, and social roles found in the major institutions of a modern social system. Thus, by internalizing standards of independence, achievement, and so forth, during their school years, individuals learn to accept and apply the norms that regulate behavior in bureaucratically organized institutions, such as the factory or the office. For present purposes, however, the primary significance of this form of socialization lies in its potential impact on students' development of functional tolerance.

As we have already seen, toleration in a pluralist democracy is thought to consist essentially of citizens' willingness to engage in fair, cooperative, goal-oriented contacts with members of out-groups. The case has also been made that these same principles underlie the policies of the U. S. government in the area of intergroup relations. According to Glazer, those laws that guarantee political and racial toleration in American life (such as the First and Fifteenth amendments and the Civil Rights Act of 1964) are ultimately rooted in moral and ethical standards of universalism, neutrality, and impartiality.[45] Hence, the norms children are believed to acquire in the course of ordinary school experience are not only consistent with, but also essential to, tolerant intergroup relations. This type of socialization would appear to be particularly effective in multiracial schools, where universalism, specificity, and achievement might have special significance for teachers and students. As pupils learn that they are judged on the basis of their performance rather than their background and that a common set of broad expectations applies to all members of the class, they come to understand that personal characteristics such as race or ethnicity are of little significance in the conduct of the school's daily routine. Furthermore, as Jackson has argued, both the crowded conditions prevailing within the classroom and the balance of power between teacher and students characteristically lead children to subordinate individualistic concerns to the general welfare.[46] In most cases, overt displays of racial antagonism (fighting, arguing, refusal to work with members of different groups) would constitute a violation of the classroom routine and would be met with relatively severe penalties. Under such circumstances, students are required to arrive at some arrangement—at very least a tenuous cease-fire—whereby teaching and learning are carried on. Finally, the very fact that the teacher is a member of a different racial group than some of the pupils in a desegregated classroom may also contribute to the child's internalization of a neutral or "color-blind" approach to social behavior. More often than not, the teacher's racial identity is of much less consequence to students than the fact that he or she has significant power over them.[47]

Of course, the extent to which students actually internalize these standards and apply them in their intergroup contacts is likely to vary greatly. For one thing, life in the classroom often proceeds along lines other than those described here. Rist, among others, has shown how teachers' biases can lead to highly particularistic treatment of pupils,[48] while Bossert's study found universalism and achievement-based evaluation to be more characteristic of some classroom situations than others.[49] Furthermore, when teacher favoritism does occur, it can have a direct negative impact on students' intergroup relations.[50] Nevertheless, if universalism is imperfectly realized in the schools, it still appears to be more typical of classroom life than does bias or favoritism. For example, in one study previously reviewed in this chapter, very few teacher behaviors were found to be directed disproportionately to one or another racial group.[51] Similar conclusions have appeared in ethnographic accounts of desegregated schools, indicating that administrators, teachers, and students tend to minimize the importance of racial identities by emphasizing color-blind policies in academic and management behavior.[52] The point is not so much that bias has disappeared from public schools as it is that as desegregation has become a fact of life in American education, universalistic, even-handed behavior has come to be expected and valued as an integral part of the school routine, and one that is essential to the maintenance of good working relationships between racial groups. In the words of Clement, Eisenhart, and Harding:

> The normative structure [of the desegregated school] tends to deemphasize the importance of social race and acts against public proclamations of suspected racism. Norms also prohibit overt racism, favoritism, and explicit reference to social race except in very restricted contexts. Norms of polite cooperation favor, at the least, an air of sociability and mutual acceptance.[53]

Thus, with the implementation of racial desegregation, the public school has come to serve as a training ground for the pragmatic, cooperative intergroup relationships that appear to be essential to the success and stability of a modern heterogeneous society. This is not to suggest, however, that children's tolerance for diversity is entirely a product of their school experience. As has already been discussed, a person's social behavior and ideology are influenced by relationships with his or her parents and exist in some rudimentary form even before the child begins school.[54] Nevertheless, most of the available evidence would seem to indicate that both the school and the home play a significant role in the socialization of tolerance, and that each institution has a "sphere of influence" in which it is primarily responsible for fostering certain types of outcomes.

SOCIALIZATION AS A DIVISION OF LABOR

Much of Durkheim's interest in public education followed from his observation of the sweeping changes in the socialization process that had resulted from the industrialization of European and American societies. In contrast with earlier ways of life, industrialization was characterized by *organic solidarity*, a condition of heightened functional differentiation and inter-dependence. Durkheim believed that as social roles grew more specialized, the family became less effective as an agency of socialization. With its diffuse functions and its intense emotional bonds, family life was not well suited to promoting the standards of duty and discipline that were required for successful participation in the new social order.[55] Instead, these capacities were seen by Durkheim as outcomes of public education:

> The schoolroom society is much closer to the society of adults than it is to that of the family . . . There is already something colder and more impersonal about the obligations imposed by the school: they are more concerned with reason and less with feelings . . . . It is by respecting the school rules that the child learns to respect rules in general, that he develops the habit of self-control and restraint simply because he should control and restrain himself. It is a first initiation into the austerity of duty. Serious life has now begun.[56]

For Durkheim, therefore, the division of labor in society at large was paralleled by the assumption of separate and distinctive roles by the school and the family as agencies of socialization. Over the years, this theme has continued to appear in the writings of social theorists. According to Parsons, socialization is a lifelong process that begins at the moment of birth with the infant's total dependency on its parents, but within which other agencies come to play an important part.[57] In the early years of life, the dependency relationship serve as a conduit for parental influence. However, it also establishes in the child's mind a linkage between satisfaction of needs or desires and the fulfillment of the expectations of other people, and it is precisely this give-and-take relationship between the self and others that forms the basis for very nearly all of the individual's future social interactions. But while the parent-child relationship represents the first stage of socialization, the role of the other is gradually expanded to include all those who have the ability to confer rewards and punishments.

With the child's entry into the school at the age of six (or thereabouts), a particularly dramatic step in the socialization process is undertaken. As Parsons and others have noted, one of the major functions of the primary school is to wean children from their families and to introduce them to the harsher realities of institutional life.[58] At school, the student as a member of a large group (i.e., the class) is treated somewhat impersonally, and is expected to comply with the relatively elaborate code of rules and regulations believed to be necessary for group life. Parsons also suggests that socialization within the schools represents a process of reality testing in which the child modifies the ideas, values, and beliefs acquired from parents in light of school experience.[59] This does not necessarily mean that the children eventually come to reject all parental beliefs. Indeed, on certain aspects of personal identity—such as religious and political affiliation—parents continue to exercise a strong influence. Rather, reality testing appears to operate on more specific questions of social belief and behavior. For example, evidence indicates that teenagers tend to differ more clearly from their parents on issues of school prayer and racial desegregation than on political party preference.[60] Given the nature of those topics, it seems likely that students' school experience has some bearing on their movement away from parental attitudes. In fact, the child's intergroup experiences within the school represent a particularly important form of reality testing. In view of continued racial segregation in housing, public schools provide students with something that is often unavailable in their homes and neighborhoods: close daily contact with children from other racial groups. As Dawson and Prewitt have noted, this elementary acquaintanceship process may have permanent effects on the child's sociopolitical development:

> [A] basic component of the political self is a set of social
> categories, identifications, and prejudices through which to fil-

ter political happenings. The development of these filters is significantly influenced by the social composition of the first major non-family group. In many instances, the school, which tries to promote social integration and toleration through a socially diversified student body, is working against the socialization of the more particularistic family.[61]

Once again, the point is not that enrollment in a desegregated school will change the child's racial attitudes, but rather that such settings provide skill and experience in cross-racial interactions. Unfortunately, there is very little evidence on the extent to which desegregated schools influence long-term social behavior. Such findings as are available, however, tend to be positive. For instance, several studies have reported a higher incidence of interracial friendships among individuals with some prior exposure to multiracial education.[62] Similarly, black students who graduated from desegregated high schools are much more likely to enroll in a predominantly white college than those who attended segregated high schools.[63]

And so, in the division of socialization between home and school, it seems reasonable to conclude that the family continues to exercise strong influence over many of the child's most basic values and beliefs, while the school functions in such a way as to acquaint the child with the realities of a complex, heterogeneous society, and, more specifically, to provide the child with the behavioral skills and dispositions that constitute functional tolerance.

TOLERANCE, UNIVERSALISM, AND "SPECIAL TREATMENT"

One factor that could influence the schools' effectiveness in promoting tolerance for diversity is the emergence of affirmative-action programs in education, government, and industry. According to some observers, the establishment of racial quotas for college and school enrollments and for employment represents a radical departure from traditional standards of universalism and neutrality in which applicants' personal backgrounds are considered irrelevant, or at least less relevant than their credentials and qualifications. Glazer, for example, has warned that school busing programs and affirmative-hiring practices intended to balance the numbers of minority students or employees set a dangerous precedent by establishing race or ethnicity as a legitimate criterion for the distribution of valued social goods. By so doing, affirmative-action programs may also inflict permanent damage on racial relations: "The greatest political consequence is undoubtedly the increasing resentment and hostility between groups that is fueled by special benefits for some."[64]

The principle that underlies affirmative action—that groups who were previously victims of discrimination should now be offered certain advantages—is also implicit in other new social programs in education. Several of these, notably multiculturalism and mainstreaming of the handicapped, will be discussed in subsequent chapters. As Glazer's argument illustrates, the selection of some groups for "special treatment" has become a point of contention not only within public education, but for American society in general. However, given the scope and complexity of this issue, it seems advisable to limit the present discussion to the possible impact of affirmative action and related programs on the socialization of tolerance.

In principle, the offering of special privileges to one group does seem to represent a violation of the universalistic standards on which public education rests. Moreover, such advantages, if interpreted as "favoritism," could undo the tentative intergroup harmony that exists in most schools. For present purposes, however, it seems important to recall that the establishment of race and ethnicity as a basis for educational policymaking was necessitated by the failure of American society to apply universalistic standards in education or, for that matter, in most other institutions. An obvious case in point is busing, which employs race as a key factor in assigning students to schools. Given the patterns of residential segregation that have long existed in many areas, the only practical way for public schools to achieve even a semblance of racial balance in enrollments has been to transport students from one section of a city or county to another. This is usually an expensive and inconvenient procedure, but it has generally proven to be a more effective means of achieving racial desegregation than the handful of other options that have been tried.[65]

The larger question, of course, is whether the benefits of desegregation are worth the price of legitimizing race as a criterion for student enrollment. From the perspective of this book, the answer can only be that they are. As has been argued, the availability of sustained daily contact between children of varying backgrounds is a prerequisite for the development of the cooperative, tolerant behavior that is essential to the well-being of a diverse, democratic society. Moreover, there is very little reason to believe that busing or other special-treatment programs have resulted in wholesale resentment and hostility *among the students themselves.* To the contrary, the evidence reviewed thus far generally points to an orderly pattern of intergroup relations in desegregated schools. This is not to deny that some potential for trouble does exist, and it is for precisely this reason that such policies must be implemented with great care.

The suggestion, then, is that absolute universalism may not always be practical or desirable. In light of our racial history and current experience, the careful, limited consideration of an individual's race, ethnicity, and other personal identifications seems, at least for the time being, a necessary step toward enhancing the schools' potential for promoting valued social outcomes. Thus, until demonstrated otherwise, this approach seems well worth the risks it entails.

CONCLUSION

As it turns out, the paradoxical relationship between education and tolerance that has been remarked on throughout these first chapters—that toleration is enhanced by exposure to virtually any quantity of formal education but is unrelated to most specific school experiences—is something of a moot issue. The strong correlation between educational attainment and tolerant attitudes seems to be partly genuine, and attributable to the "cultural sophistication" of the well-educated, and partly an artifact, created by researchers' use of transparent measures that inflate the true correlation and lead to underestimates of the effectiveness of socialization mechanisms within the school. But the larger issue surrounding this line of inquiry is the likelihood that abstract, symbolic racial and political attitudes have little bearing on the realities of toleration in modern societies. It was suggested that a more suitable focus for research is the individual's willingness to accept the human variation encountered in real-life situations. Furthermore, this pattern of functional tolerance was seen as a probable outcome of children's school experiences. It was argued that when norms of fairness and impartiality are learned in an integrated classroom, they provide the social-psychological foundations for cooperative working relationships between diverse groups.

While this chapter has offered some ideas for moving beyond the present impasse in tolerance research, it also raises more questions than it answers. Among the major issues that require clarification is the relationship between the normative and behavioral components of functional tolerance. That is, does a child's acquisition of universalistic standards lead to more frequent and favorable intergroup contacts, and vice versa? Similarly, it seems important to expand current inquiries into the factors that influence cross-racial interactions among students. As noted previously, there has been some real progress in this area, but these studies remain relatively rare. In regard to generalizability, attention should be directed to the possibility that tolerance in the classroom eventually has spillover effects into other institutions.

On the whole then, it would seem that research has barely begun to examine the ways in which public schools influence children's racial relations, and, more generally, their tolerance for diversity. Clearly, the child's acquisition of functional tolerance is an important form of learning and, as such, is part of the broader process of social development.

4

An Analytic Framework for Students' Intergroup Relations

With the approach of the thirtieth anniversary of the Supreme Court's *Brown* v. *Board of Education* ruling, racial desegregation has become a well-established fact of life in American education. Although some of the original objectives of school desegregation have not been achieved, including equalization of academic performance of blacks and whites, the U. S. Commission on Civil Rights has concluded that "desegregation works," at least to the extent that "most citizens feel that compliance with the law is in the best interests of their children and their communities."[1] This conclusion is similar to the point advanced in chapter 3 that public schools are generally successful in promoting functional tolerance among students.

Functional tolerance is, as we have seen, a pattern of orderly, cooperative, but limited contact between members of diverse groups. As such, it falls well short of the genuine integration that some proponents of desegregation had hoped would be achieved in the multiracial school. On the other hand, it is certainly preferable to the outright racial conflict that had once been predicted by opponents of desegregation. But despite the mounting evidence that it is this intermediate pattern of inter-group relations, rather than either of the two extremes, that is most characteristic of desegregated schools, surprisingly little effort has been made to explore the antecedents and conse-quences of functional tolerance. Instead, it seems almost to have been taken for granted that black, white, and other students will gradually learn to get along reasonably well with each other, and that such arrangements as are made will have little direct bearing on other types of socialization outcomes.

This chapter offers another way of looking at children's experiences in multiracial schools. Specifically, students' acquisi-tion of functional tolerance represents an important form of social learning that is best understood as part of the overall process of social development. Of particular interest is the pos-sibility that children's intergroup relations correspond to the various levels of moral development identified by Lawrence Kohlberg and his associates. By applying this approach, we may gain a clearer basis for investigating and eventually understand-ing the dynamics of children's intergroup relations.

MORAL DEVELOPMENT

For Kohlberg, moral growth essentially consists of the indi-vidual's gradual acquisition of general social values, and his or her willingness to apply those values to judgments and be-haviors.[2] In contrast with the position that children's social learning occurs haphazardly, Kohlberg posits the existence of "stages or directed structural age-changes in the area of social personality,"[3] which are very similar to the stages of cognitive development identified by the Swiss psychologist Jean Piaget. And although moral behavior may be strongly influenced by cognition, the two are best thought of as distinct, parallel areas of development.[4] Specifically, there are three broad develop-mental levels, each characterized by a different basis for moral judgment. At the *preconventional* level, judgments are externally motivated, that is, guided by an overriding concern for the physical consequences of an action, particularly rewards and punishments. *Conventional* morality is characterized by performance of roles, maintenance of routines, and meeting the expectations of others. Finally, *postconventional* moral values reside in the individual's conformity to general standards, rights, and duties.[5] Hence, as persons move from a purely egoistic orientation based on satisfaction of immediate needs and wants to a concern for the greater good, they acquire conscience and a sense of principle. In short, they become more fully moral.

Moral stage theory was originally concerned with the child's acquisition of social ethics, such as the rightness or wrongness of cheating or stealing. By constructing hypothetical dilemmas and locating subjects' resolutions along a hierarchical scale of principles, Kohlberg sought to classify respondents into six moral stages (two stages at each of the three levels of development). Perhaps the best known of these imaginary dilemmas is the case of Heinz, who steals a drug needed to save the life of his desperately ill wife. At the lower developmental stages, subjects' judgments about the propriety of Heinz's action tend to emphasize "irrelevant physical forms" of the theft, for example, the value of the object stolen, or its direct consequences (the effect of the theft on others who might need the drug). Conventional judgments are based on role expectations, such as the responsibility of a husband to his wife, or the wrongness of theft under any circumstances. By contrast, postconventional interpretations center on Heinz's need to choose between two conflicting moral principles—the value of life versus the value of law.[6]

In recent years, research on moral stage theory has been extended to include many facets of children's sociopolitical development. According to Kohlberg, "moral and civic education are much the same thing . . . . Civic or political education means the stimulation of more advanced patterns of reasoning about social and political decisions and their interpretation in action. These patterns are patterns of moral reasoning."[7] The expanding research on this model generally shows it to be a good predictor of an individual's social judgments. One study by Tapp and Kohlberg found that subjects' views of the functions of law within society were differentiated according to levels of moral development. Preconventional subjects saw legal compliance as a means for suppressing evil and for avoiding punishment; those at the conventional stages held the law to be a guide for normal expected behavior and a basis for dealing fairly with other people; and postconventionals stressed the common good as the rationale underlying legal codes.[8] Similarly, in applying this theory to children's tolerance for diversity, Davidson found that students' frequency of expression of negative racial/ethnic sentiments was inversely related to their level of moral development.[9]

In light of these and other findings,[10] it seems likely that Kohlberg's developmental model can be profitably applied to students' intergroup relations. Just as moral stage theory sees children's judgments as manifestations of different social standards, so too do students' interracial contacts usually reflect certain norms and values.

VARIETIES OF INTERGROUP BEHAVIOR

Intergroup behavior refers to patterns of overt, observable interaction that occur between members of the major racial groups within a school enrollment. Of particular interest are two properties of the contact situation: first, the direction of interactions; second, the purpose or underlying motivation of participants. For convenience, we will classify the direction of interactions as either positive or negative. *Positive* contacts include any interactions in which favorable sentiment (friendship, acceptance, etc.), is expressed or implied, as well as those neutral exchanges that are sometimes required of students. *Negative* interactions are those in which unfavorable sentiments (anger, hostility, aggression) are expressed or implied and that violate the traditional codes of student conduct or the color-blind policies that pertain within many desegregated schools (see Chapter 3). One potential problem area in this system is the classification of noninteractions or avoidance between groups. According to some observers, avoidance represents a form of racism;[11] others, however, feel that a certain degree of preference for one's own group is inevitable, and, in some circumstances, constitutes an expression more of racial pride than of hostility.[12] For present purposes, a pattern of avoidance will be classified as negative only if it interferes with the normal routines of school and classroom life. Thus if blacks and whites refuse to participate in racially mixed work groups, we may safely classify this as negative behavior. In purely voluntary situations however (such as friendship choices or lunchroom seating), racial clustering is more neutral than negative, and under this system classified as positive. The second dimension of an interaction is the actor's purpose or motivation. Here, the Kohlberg scheme will be adapted to produce three conditions: preconventional behavior—in which actors are oriented to the immediate consequences of their actions, specifically to rewards and punishments; conventional behavior—characterized by participants' orientation toward norms and role expectations; postconventional behavior—in which participants are guided by some general value.

With three levels for each of the two directions, the total classification system consists of six categories of intergroup interaction. These categories are summarized in table 4.1 below. Let us consider each in greater detail.

TABLE 4.1: Types of Intergroup Behavior

MOTIVATION OF PARTICIPANTS:	DIRECTION	
	POSITIVE	NEGATIVE
Preconventional	Compliance	Random disturbance
Conventional	Functional tolerance	Discrimination
Postconventional	Integration	Conflict

Positive Interactions

Compliance is a minimally acceptable pattern of intergroup contact. It describes a tenuous state of nonbelligerence that is grounded solely in pupils' desire to avoid the penalties that would follow from their displays of racial hostility. Under this condition, voluntary cross-racial interactions, let alone friendships, are infrequent, and such contact as does occur tends to be formalized and limited to specific tasks. In other words, students are willing to carry out their role responsibilities in racially mixed settings (e.g., participate in work groups), but no more than that. Obviously, such a racial climate leaves much to be desired. It is however, relatively uncommon, and occurs mainly in the early stages of a desegregation program. Orfield writes of the crisis period that sometimes follows the implementation of desegregation. As students become accustomed to the new arrangement, their intergroup relations move toward normalization.[13]

In most schools, normalization means *functional tolerance*. Because this pattern of interaction has already been described at length in chapter 3, we need only review its highlights here. Briefly, intergroup relations of this type are marked by "polite cooperation"[14] and stem from the informal code of color-blindness found within desegregated schools. Behavior is shaped primarily by students' desire to fulfill the expectations of teachers and classmates that racial identity will be ignored or deemphasized. A functionally tolerant climate may succeed in suppressing racial hostilities and in stabilizing school routines through informal but consistent enforcement of clear norms for intergroup behavior. On the other hand, cross-racial interactions usually take the form of working relationships, and tend to be most successful when supervised by adults.[15] Thus, intergroup socializing and friendships are infrequent. The strong role orientations found among students in a functionally tolerant school are indicative of the conventional level of moral development.

For many proponents of desgregation, the ultimate goal of

multiracial education is true *integration*. Integration has been achieved only when racial identification plays no significant part in either the formal or informal routines of the school. In a truly integrated school environment, each racial group participates on an approximately equal basis in the classes, activities, rewards, punishments, and interactions that constitute school life. Cross-racial contacts are as frequent, friendly, and diffuse in purpose as those that occur within a group. Integration cannot be mandated or imposed by school authorities, but is instead the result of students' acceptance of positive racial values (such as the equality and brotherhood/sisterhood of all human beings). Thus, integration reflects a postconventional level of moral orientation. However, the available research indicates that postconventional morality in general and true integration in particular are rarely achieved.[16] In fact, about the only places where the behavioral manifestations of integration are much in evidence are primary-grade classrooms. There, however, children's relationships are based more on obliviousness to racial differentiation than on understanding or acceptance of racial values. Accordingly, even the most successful multiracial primary classes cannot be said to be truly integrated in the sense that this term is used here.

Negative Interactions

Given the troubled history of intergroup relations in the United States, and the persistence of severe social and economic inequality today, it is probably inevitable that racial tension would find its way into the public schools. Although American education has generally experienced an orderly movement toward racial desegregation, there have been instances of strong, even violent, resistance to desegregation. Even today, nearly thirty years after *Brown* v. *Board of Education*, racial antagonism remains commonplace in some schools. Certainly the most publicized trouble spot in recent years has been Boston. While overt conflict has been relatively short-lived elsewhere, the situation in parts of Boston appears to be one of enduring hostility. For instance, during a single month in Fall 1979, the sixth year of that city's desegregation program, the following events were reported:

> Racial fighting broke out as students waited to pass through the metal detectors that guarded the entrances to South Boston High School.
>
> At East Boston High, a white pupil was stabbed by a black schoolmate.
>
> On the same day a gang of white high school students attacked a black couple on Boston Common, a white teacher was assaulted by black youths outside Roxbury High School.
>
> During a football game at Charlestown High School, a visiting player was shot and critically wounded. The victim was black, and the alleged assailants white.[17]

The origins of these and similar incidents lie outside the school and, in particular, in the system of racial stratification that remains in place in the United States. However, school desegregation programs sometimes exacerbate racial tensions by placing contending or hostile groups in close physical proximity under less-than-ideal conditions, as was apparently the case in Boston. Given the furor that has attended some school desegregation efforts, it should not be surprising that racial conflict receives more attention when it occurs in the school than in other institutions. Therefore, even though overtly negative interactions seem to be quite unusual in most desegregated schools,[18] it seems important that every effort be made to understand those that do occur.

Based upon the participants' underlying motivation, negative interaction patterns between white and minority pupils may be categorized into three broad types. *Random disturbances* are usually minor episodes. Because school buildings contain very large numbers of children and adolescents for extended periods of time, interpersonal conflict is bound to occur. The law of averages would suggest that in a desegregated school, some of these encounters will involve pupils of different racial backgrounds. Such episodes should not be presumed to be racial in origin or intent. Displays of purely personal hostility between members of different groups may be described as random disturbances, in that they are isolated and nonrepetitive, and usually have no wider effect on intergroup relations. Underlying motives or racial attitudes are not a factor here, and the only standards that are violated are the school's ordinary rules of conduct. In all likelihood, the majority of negative cross-racial interactions among students fall into this category. But while these disturbances are in themselves inconsequential, they may have some potential for escalating intergroup tensions.

Discrimination occurs when students violate norms of fairness in dealing with members of other racial groups. The issue here is not some purely personal preference (such as friendship or companionship), but rather the denial of status to a qualified person solely on the grounds of race. For example, Collins has described cases in which individuals were excluded from participation in extracurricular activities (cheerleading, ROTC) largely on the basis of their racial "style."[19] Unlike the other negative interaction patterns, discrimination involves no physical confrontation between members of different groups. It is instead a more subtle, although no less potentially provocative, manifestation of intergroup tension.

Conflict is the most serious and least frequent type of negative cross-racial interaction. This pattern includes any specific behaviors motivated by racial hatred or hostility, and is graphically exemplified by the events in Boston described earlier in this chapter.

Once again, these categories are intended as broad types, and may not include all of the varieties of negative contact found within schools. In addition, some incidents may fit into more than one pattern, such as an initially trivial personal encounter that flares into widespread racial fighting or a racially motivated action that turns out to be inconsequential.

However useful these categories may be in describing students' intergroup patterns, they in themselves do not fully explain why such behaviors occur. In addition to students' own motivations, the climates and structures of the school help to determine what goes on there.

SCHOOL'S INFLUENCE ON INTERGROUP RELATIONS: PROPOSITIONS AND PROCEDURES FOR RESEARCH

In chapter 3, it was suggested that public schools provide students with opportunities for cooperative intergroup contact and regulate these contacts through unwritten but powerful norms of color blindness or universalism. Together, these norms and behaviors are the essence of functional tolerance. I will now extend the argument by suggesting that not only functional tolerance but also the other varieties of cross-racial interaction are influenced by the social structures and normative climates of the school and classroom. These relationships are outlined in figure 4.A. As can be seen in this greatly simplified diagram, the school's structural and normative characteristics (stage 1) are believed to influence students' intergroup behaviors (stage 3) directly and indirectly (through pupils' internalization of school norms—stage 2). Each of these stages, of course, actually consists of a number of specific structural, normative, or behavioral measures.

FIGURE 4.A: A Model of the School's Influence on Students' Intergroup Behaviors

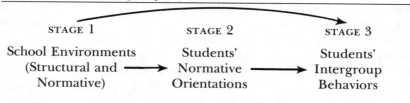

STAGE 1	STAGE 2	STAGE 3
School Environments (Structural and Normative)	Students' Normative Orientations	Students' Intergroup Behaviors

Stage 1—School Environments

STRUCTURES. Social structure is generally conceived of as any regular and recurring pattern of interaction. Within schools, there are countless policies and practices that are essentially structural in nature in that they define the conditions and settings for interaction among students or between students and teachers. By so doing, these policies also have important implications for interracial contact. At a minimum, intergroup behavior requires some degree of physical proximity. Thus, any policy that requires the placement of white and minority pupils within the same setting increases the likelihood of cross-racial interaction. Examples include policies mandating racial balance in school and/or classroom enrollments. Within the classroom, teachers can devise seating arrangements that reduce students' tendencies toward racial clustering.[20] Likewise, the use of racially balanced cooperative work groups appears to be one of the better predictors of black-white contacts. Open-classroom techniques emphasize freedom of movement and communication among pupils, and therefore have the side effect of raising the level of cross-racial interaction.[21]

While all of these devices promote physical proximity, they also may facilitate interracial contact by reducing psychological barriers between groups. As Schofield and Sagar have argued, proximity enhances acquaintanceship and familiarity.[22] For children, as for adults, it is usually much easier to talk with someone who is known through close daily contacts. On the whole, then, it can be expected that structural variables of the type described here will increase intergroup interaction by providing the physical and psychological prerequisites for these contacts.

NORMATIVE CLIMATES. The term *normative climates* will be used to describe any standards within the school and classroom that pertain directly or indirectly to students' intergroup relations and the degree to which they are enforced.

Such standards are considered to be properties of the school environment that exist independently of individual actors. These standards may take the form of *rules of conduct*, which mandate or proscribe specific actions; *norms*, which identify appropriate types of behaviors for different statuses and roles; and *values*, which are highly generalized conceptions of worth.[23]

Each type of standard has been found to have a distinctive influence on intergroup relations. Rules of conduct are important in preventing overt displays of hostility and in maintaining school and classroom routines. While some questions have been raised about the "cultural bias" implicit in traditional disciplinary policies,[24] discipline or rule enforcement is usually one of the foremost objectives of newly desegregated schools, and, according to some observers, is a prerequisite for successful desegregation.[25] Norms differ from rules in several respects. Whereas rules are directly stated and refer to specific actions, norms are implicit within situations and describe the *patterns* of behavior expected of role-incumbents (e.g., teachers or students). We have already discussed in some detail the ways in which norms of universalism, fairness, and neutrality govern intergroup behavior in schools. Particularly important in this regard are the color-blind policies underlying teacher-student interactions and the assumptions of "normal progression" in pupil-to-pupil intergroup dealings.[26] In comparison with both rules and norms, general racial values play a lesser role within the school's normative climate. For one thing, values (such as racial equality and human brotherhood) are more centrally located within individual personalities[27] and are therefore more difficult to transmit, change, or enforce. Since values tend to be somewhat abstractly formulated, they may have less direct bearing on specific behaviors than do rules and norms. Thus, while positive racial values are desirable, they are not essential to the success of a desegregation program. For example, teachers who are scrupulously even-handed may be motivated more by professional ethics than by deeply felt social ideals. Similarly, regardless of their general beliefs about race relations or integration, most teachers will want to enforce order and discipline in their classrooms. Nevertheless, racial values can and sometimes do influence patterns of behavior within the school. On the negative side, we have already seen how the racial hostility in various parts of Boston found expression in several schools. Conversely, the very positive value and interaction patterns of some schools occasionally appear in desegregation evaluations and field reports.[28]

Stage 2—Students' Normative Orientations

While normative climates are properties of the school environment, normative orientations are characteristics of individuals. In particular, they describe the extent to which students' intergroup behaviors are guided by rules of conduct, norms, or general racial values. As discussed previously, students at the preconventional level of development are attuned mainly to precise rules and regulations. Thus, they comply with the regulations governing behavior, or occasionally violate those rules. In neither their positive nor their negative cross-racial contacts do norms and values come into play. Conventional-level students, on the other hand, are more aware of the norms for appropriate intergroup behavior. Thus, a sense of fairness and color blindness may shape their positive interactions. However, students at this stage may also violate these standards by engaging in deliberate acts of discrimination. Finally, there are a handful of postconventional-level students whose behaviors are shaped by strong social values. When their values are positive, interactions conform to the ideals of true integration—that is, race is simply not a factor in work relationships, friendships, social activities, and so forth. On the other hand, it can be assumed that some of the acts of racial violence discussed previously were carried out by individuals holding extremely negative racial values.

One factor that should be considered in assessing normative orientations is the age level of the students. As Kohlberg's work clearly demonstrates, significant and consistent differences exist among the moral (or, in our term, normative) orientations of very young children (characteristically preconventional), preadolescents (conventional), and adolescents (also conventional, but with greater frequency of postconventionalism).[29] Thus, the seeming disregard for racial identification often displayed by primary-grade youngsters cannot be classified as integration, since it is unlikely to be based on a postconventional normative orientation (conscious acceptance of positive racial values). On the other hand, it is reasonable to assume that when a similar condition is found in the high school, it stems from the advanced level of moral development among students.

Stage 3—Students' Intergroup Behavior

With the heightened interest in school desegregation in the years since the *Brown* decision, researchers have pursued a variety of approaches to the study of students' cross-racial interactions, including sociometric surveys, detailed observational systems, and ethnographic techniques. Typically, the major dependent variables in these studies have been the frequency and direction of the contacts. In addition, the locus or source of instigation (e.g., teacher, minority pupil, or white pupil) and the purpose of the interaction (social or academic, general or specific) have received some attention.

In most cases, these variables can be assessed fairly easily, and do not require much interpretation on the part of the observer. This is also true of most of the structural variables (grouping or seating practices, enrollment policies, etc.) that are included in stage 1 of the model. However, the remaining sets of variables—the normative climates of schools (also stage 1) and the normative orientations of students (stage 2)—do not lend themselves so readily to observation and analysis. Here it may be necessary to probe beneath the surface of behaviors to determine the influence of rules, norms, and values. Let us consider more closely the steps involved in this type of analysis.

A NOTE ON METHOD: THE PROCESS OF NORMATIVE INFERENCE

In attempting to determine the influence of various sets of standards on students' intergroup behaviors, we are confronted with a two-step task: first, describing the rules, norms, and values that characterize a school setting (i.e., the normative climate); second, determining the extent to which students have internalized those standards and applied them to their own cross-racial relations. Throughout this process, the research will, of course, be required to distinguish carefully between normative climates and normative orientations. Separation of environmental and individual characteristics has long been a challenge to social scientists. According to one commentator, approaches to this problem have generally proceeded along two lines. The "subjective" method entails the aggregation of individual properties to form an environmental indicator, while the "objective" approach utilizes characteristics of the environment itself that are not reducible to individual characteristics.[30] As will be evident shortly, both procedures have something to contribute to the study of the school's influence on intergroup relations.

Another problem stems from the nature of social standards. While specific rules of student conduct may be formally proclaimed (verbally and/or in writing), such is usually not true of norms and values. Thus, to describe both normative climates (of the school or classroom) and normative orientations (of students), researchers will be required to infer relevant standards by studying both social environments and individual behaviors. For both levels of analysis, the normative inference process will consist of steps similar to those described by Williams: (1) recording the testimony of individuals, through interviews or questionnaires, as to the values they hold and the norms they follow in given situations; (2) studying choices of objects or actions either in natural settings or in tests, interviews, or experiments; (3) studying directions of interest or emphasis through documentary analysis or behavioral observation; (4) observing the distribution of rewards and punishments in actual situations.[31]

Some of these procedures do not require direct contact between researchers and students, which, in a tense or highly charged racial climate, is an advantage. Nevertheless, to identify students' norms and values, some personal contact with subjects, in the form of interviews or questionnaire administration, seems inevitable. The problem with the inference of norms from pupil behavior alone is that it puts the investigator in a bind: If certain cross-racial interactions serve as the dependent variable (or stage 3) in an analysis, they cannot also be used as measures of the independent or mediating variable, that is, the students' normative orientation (stage 2). To illustrate, suppose we find that students regularly display friendliness and fairness in their intergroup transactions, and we duly record observations of a positive racial contact. We may not use these same observations as a basis for inferring that those students have a universalistic normative orientation. Instead, evidence of students' acceptance of those norms must be gathered independently, either through direct testimony or through observation of behavior in other contexts.

The problem of tautology also arises in aggregating individual data to form measures of the normative climates of schools. Just as it is impermissible to use a single observation as an indicator of both motivation and behavior, so we cannot use an observation as a measure of both normative climate (an environmental characteristic) and normative orientations (which are traits of individuals). However, other types of aggregate data (especially those gathered through teachers' or administrators' testimony and through the observation of their behavior) are entirely legitimate measures of the school or classroom climate. This subjective approach to institutional analyses was utilized in several ethnographic studies of desegregated schools, which used interviews with teachers to reveal the existence of pervasive but informal norms concerning student-teacher interactions and students' intergroup relations.[32] The objective method, entailing the use of global measures, might also be applied to gain a wide range of information about the school's normative climate. Among the numerous techniques available are analysis of school documents (letters to parents, memoranda to teachers, written codes of conduct, etc.), interviews with knowledgeable sources about the school's racial history and the overall pattern of race relations in the community, observation of the school's physical environment (posters, decorations, displays), and observation of Parent-Teacher Association meetings and other social functions.

By way of summarizing this section, table 4.2 outlines the most important indicators of the variables at each stage of the research model, and the procedures for gathering information on each indicator.

LONG-TERM OUTCOMES

Finally, the possibility should be considered that children's experiences in desegregated schools have long-term effects on their intergroup relations. As we have already seen, and will see again in subsequent chapters, the ultimate goal of the so-called social-engineering programs within the school is the promotion of integration, cohesion, and stability in American society at large. As a result of their school experiences, children are expected to learn to perform successfully in the institutions of a heterogeneous society and also to become more tolerant of human diversity in general. Another way of stating this is to suggest that the implicit social lessons of the desegregated classroom are intended to have both *lateral* and *vertical* generalizability. According to Breer and Locke,[33] lateral generalizability occurs when individuals internalize the normative content of certain experiences and subsequently apply it to situations that closely resemble the original. Norms are generalized vertically when they are accepted as values, and applied as overall guides to behaviors and judgments.

The basic requirement for research on this issue would be the long-term analysis of intergroup behaviors and normative orientations of individuals with substantial exposure to multiracial schooling, as compared with alumni of more homogeneous

TABLE 4.2: Variables, Indicators, and Research Techniques for Studying Schools' Influence on Students' Intergroup Relations

SCHOOL AND CLASSROOM ENVIRONMENTS	STUDENTS' NORMATIVE ORIENTATIONS	STUDENTS' INTERGROUP BEHAVIORS

STRUCTURES
 	
Indicators:
Management policies
Instructional practices
 	
Research Techniques:
Observation
Documentary analysis
Direct testimony
 	
NORMATIVE CLIMATES
 	
Indicators:
Existence and enforcement of
  Rules
  Norms
  Values
 	
Research Techniques:
Observation
Documentary analysis
Direct testimony
	Indicators:
	Acceptance/
	rejection of
	  Rules
	  Norms
	  Values
	
	Research Techniques:
	Observation
	Indirect testimony
		Indicators:
		Frequency
		Direction
		Locus of
		  instigation
		Purpose
		
		Research Techniques:
		Observation

schools. The procedures for behavioral observation and normative inference among these groups would essentially be the same as those described in the previous discussion, except that the focal point of this research would shift from schools to the major institutions of adult life, especially the work place. There are, however, problems in conducting studies of this type. Conceptually, it may seem unreasonable to attribute adults' behaviors and beliefs to the socialization patterns of their school years. In a more technical vein, many adults might not be able to recall their school experiences with any real accuracy. Yet, research evidence suggests the contrary on both points. First, it is known that childhood socialization does have a strong, enduring influence on individuals' orientations toward diversity, although there remains disagreement about the precise nature and magnitude of that influence. (See, for example, the discussion of *The Authoritarian Personality* in chapter 2.) Second, adults often have surprisingly vivid recollections of certain noteworthy classroom socialization practices. Almond and Verba found that politically effective adults recalled active participation in classroom decision making,[34] while another study discovered that one subsample of adult respondents was able to recall in great detail a particular first-grade teacher who appeared to have had a unique and enduring influence on her former students.[35] Therefore, given the evidently powerful impressions that some childhood experiences make on adults, it seems likely that a retrospective analysis centering on so sensitive an issue as school desegregation would be entirely feasible.

CONCLUSION

This brief outline of an analytic framework for students' intergroup relations concludes the effort to show how the traditional features of the school and classroom contribute to the child's development of tolerance for diversity. The point has been made that much of the most effective training that desegregated schools provide occurs not as a result of deliberate policies, but instead as a consequence of routine instructional practices and interactions between teachers and students, and between students themselves. It may seem ironic, then, that American educators have in recent years adopted several new programs designed explicitly to promote social tolerance. These policies, particularly multicultural education and mainstreaming of the handicapped, are at the present time too new to permit systematic assessment of their effects. They do, however, warrant at least tentative examination.

5

Mainstreaming the Handicapped

In November 1975, President Gerald R. Ford signed into law the Education for All Handicapped Children Act (P. L. 94-142).[1] Among the major provisions of the new legislation were the following:

- As of 1980, free public education is to be made available to all handicapped children between the ages of 3 and 21.
- Every handicapped student is entitled to an "individualized educational plan," jointly developed by teachers, parents, school officials, and whenever possible, by the student.
- Prior consultation with parents is required for the implementation of any decision concerning the education of a handicapped child.
- Handicapped students must be educated in the "least restrictive environment," including regular public school classrooms, should such placement be deemed consistent with the needs of the student.

P.L. 94-142, and particularly its "least restrictive environment" clause, serves as the basis for one of the most important and most controversial issues in public education today—the integration of physically, mentally, and emotionally handicapped students within regular classrooms. While this policy, commonly known as "mainstreaming,"[2] is not required by P.L. 94-142, this law has certainly had the effect of encouraging regular class placement. In 1977, for instance, nearly 2.5 million handicapped students were receiving all or part of their schooling in regular classes.[3] Barring unforeseen problems, this number will increase steadily as teachers, students, and parents become accustomed to the new policy.

In the comparatively short period of time since the passage of P.L. 94-142, mainstreaming has become the subject of considerable discussion and debate. Among the major questions that have been raised are the effects of this policy on the academic routines of the regular classroom and on the scholastic performances and psychological orientations of the exceptional student. In this chapter, we will focus on another issue, which has hitherto received relatively little attention, namely, the potential impact of mainstreaming on the socialization of nonhandicapped pupils. Quite clearly, exceptional students represent a significant and often highly visible minority group within some classrooms. In addition, their specialized educational needs may set them even further apart from their normal peers. How the nonhandicapped child reacts to this new situation could conceivably affect his or her own orientations not only to the handicapped, but also to the overall realities of social diversity.

To some extent, mainstreaming can be viewed as one more manifestation of the increasingly diversified character of public school enrollments. Over the past ten or fifteen years, a number of changes have taken place that have made the typical student body more broadly representative of the overall national population. For example, school consolidations in rural areas and small towns have resulted in vastly expanded attendance zones. By drawing their enrollments from wider areas, schools increase the diversity found within their student bodies. In addition, some of the separate school systems that have served particular social groups have recently begun to diminish in size—Native American pupils appear to be gradually abandoning the federally supported reservation schools, and growing proportions of Catholic students are now enrolled in public schools.[4] (A counter-trend in the form of increased enrollments in the "Christian academies" and other schools affiliated with Protestant churches will be discussed in chapter 7.) Finally, and most significantly, black children have gradually been incorporated into the educational mainstream. With the elimination of strict racial dualism in the South, and the restriction of de facto segregation elsewhere, ever-increasing numbers of black students are now attending schools that have at least some degree of racial balance.[5] Indeed, as a vehicle for social integration, the current trend toward mainstreaming of the handicapped closely parallels the policy of racial desegregation. In particular, each is based on roughly the same historical, legal, and sociological foundations. Therefore, to gain a clearer perspective on mainstreaming, it may be helpful to explore its similarity to the slightly earlier effort to integrate black children into the public schools.

BLACK EDUCATION AND EDUCATION OF THE HANDICAPPED

In the early years of this century, schooling was regarded as something of a luxury. Only about 70 percent of all children between the ages of five and seventeen were formally enrolled in schools, and even fewer actually attended on a regular basis.[6] According to the popular view, the child best able to benefit from education was typically a middle- or upper-class boy who was bound for one of the professions. The energies of most other youngsters were expected to be put to good use around the home, the farm, or the factory. By the 1970s, however, all of this had changed. Enrollment of school-age children had long since become compulsory, and the vast majority of students were staying around long enough to earn their high school diplomas.[7] Education had become, in a word, *inclusive*.

This same term can be used to describe the increasing educational attainments of both black and handicapped Americans. In addition, more and more of these pupils have come to be enrolled in the same schools attended by white, nonhandicapped children. In general, this progression can be seen to have occurred in three separate stages.[8]

The first and longest stage was a period of isolation or, at best, marginal inclusion, which lasted through the mid-1950s. During this period, the segregation of both blacks and the handicapped was extensive, but not absolute. In general, little attention was paid to the educational needs of either group. In many rural areas, children with certain handicapping conditions, such as mild retardation or physical impairment, may have been routinely enrolled in regular classes, while the more severely handicapped were directed to residential schools and institutions, or were entirely neglected by public agencies. Federal legislation and guidelines for the education of the handicapped were virtually nonexistent at this time, and state laws were more often permissive (allowing localities to make their own provisions for special education) than mandatory. A similar pattern characterized the education of black children during the first half of the century. While dual school systems were legally authorized only in southern and border states, various forms of de facto segregation (particularly the manipulation of school attendance zones to coincide with boundaries of racially homogeneous neighborhoods) were common in the North and effectively resulted in the exclusion of the vast majority of black pupils from schools attended by whites. Such practices were not only regarded as socially desirable, but were also consistent with the prevailing legal principle of "separate but equal," set forth by the U.S. Supreme Court in *Plessy* v. *Ferguson*.[9] In most cases, of course, only the first part of this principle was honored. While segregation was enthusiastically practiced, dramatic disparities existed in the quality of schooling provided to blacks and whites, as evidenced in the vastly different levels of per capita funding provided for dual school systems in many states.[10]

The second stage in the educational histories of both blacks and the handicapped can be characterized as a period of expanding legal entitlement. Beginning in the 1950s, the federal government began to take greater notice of the educational rights of both groups. One of the first significant actions taken to improve special education came in 1958 with the passage of P.L. 85-926, which was aimed at increasing the number of teachers of the mentally retarded. Further steps were taken during the early 1960s, when Congress enacted P.L. 88-164, which extended the provisions of the earlier law to address the needs of other handicapped children, and P.L. 89-750, which created the Bureau of Education for the Handicapped. According to a number of observers, the primary significance of these laws lay in their establishment of a strong federal interest and involvement in the education of handicapped children.[11] Finally, the right of the handicapped to public education was argued, very often successfully, in a series of class-action cases in lower federal courts. For example, *Pennsylvania Association for Retarded Children* v. *Pennsylvania*[12] produced a consent agreement in which that state agreed to assume responsibility for providing public education to all retarded children.

The legal entitlement of black children to attend schools previously closed to them was established in principle by the U.S. Supreme Court in *Brown* v. *Board of Education*.[13] Although this ruling clearly prohibited *de jure* segregation, its immediate impact was felt only in those border states (and the District of Columbia) that chose to dismantle their dual systems in compliance with the Court's mandate. Substantially unaffected until much later were the various forms of de facto segregation practiced in the North and West, as well as the dual school systems of the South, which were able to forestall desegregation under the *Brown* ruling's ambiguous provision that segregation be ended "with all deliberate speed." Thus, while equal educational opportunity for blacks was far from being realized during this period, the *Brown* decision was a key first step toward this end. Furthermore, within the next dozen years, Congress passed a series of laws—in particular, P.L. 89-10, the Elementary and Secondary Education Act of 1965—in which educational funding provisions enabled the executive branch of the federal government to enforce compliance with *Brown*.

The 1970s signaled the third step in the advancement of educational opportunities for blacks and the handicapped, and are best described as a period of active movement toward the integration of both groups. During the first part of the decade, the desirability of separate facilities for the education of the handicapped was challenged in research findings[14] and in a series of class-action cases. One critical aspect of these suits, most of which dealt with the placement of minority children in special classes, was the contention that education for the handicapped was inferior to regular education and led to irreparable psychological harm. The shift in public sentiment away from special class placement was further manifested in several key pieces of legislation enacted by Congress at this time. While these laws (most notably P.L. 93-380) symbolized an ever-increasing federal commitment to the education of the handicapped, they have since been overshadowed by P.L. 94-142, whose "least restrictive environment" clause has effectively resulted in the inclusion of hundreds of thousands of exceptional children within regular classrooms.

Noteworthy trends in racial desegregation during the 1970s included the virtual elimination of racial dualism in southern school districts and the extension of the integration effort to the North and West. The dramatic turnabout in the South is best evidenced by the decline in the proportion of minority pupils attending segregated schools (i.e., those with less than 1 percent white enrollment) from 64 percent in 1968 to 14 percent in 1972.[15] Extensive desegregation efforts have begun more recently in a number of northeastern and midwestern cities, but may be limited by the increasing abandonment of central city schools by the white middle class and by the Supreme Court's reluctance to prescribe interdistrict desegregation.[16]

While the parallels between the two movements seem clear, there are also important differences, particularly with regard to implementation. For one thing, mainstreaming has been initiated with fewer delays and with less overt resistance than was racial desegregation. This may be attributed, in part, to the fact that the Supreme Court did not mandate a specific schedule for the elimination of segregation, and delegated enforcement to lower federal courts, while P.L. 94-142 contains specific provisions (and deadlines) for full compliance. Also, resistance to racial desegregation was based on long-standing customs and beliefs, while opposition to mainstreaming requirements has stemmed principally from concerns over practical problems. Unlike racial integration, which has generally required relatively few changes in instructional practice, the integration of handicapped children has brought about extensive revisions in the daily routines of the school and classroom. These adjustments include the adaptation of physical environments, the development of individual educational programs, the provision of special equipment, and the acquisition of a broad range of new skills by teachers. It is, in fact, the extensiveness of change within the classroom that appears to be the basis for some educators' resistance to mainstreaming. This is, in a sense, a hopeful sign, since it should be easier to provide the human and material resources needed in the mainstreamed classroom than to change deeply rooted social customs, as has sometimes been required for racial desegregation. It might be anticipated, therefore, that if P.L. 94-142 and accompanying state and local legislation are implemented carefully, opposition to mainstreaming may diminish fairly quickly.

THE INTEGRATION MANDATES: SOCIAL AND LEGAL FOUNDATIONS

So far, this analysis has addressed the coincidence of separate developments in special education and the education of black Americans. However, the recent advances in each field can be seen as closely interrelated parts of a broader movement toward social integration. More precisely, the mainstreaming movement owes much of its success to the changing conceptions of equality of opportunity that emerged from *Brown* v. *Board of Education.* The major points of that ruling were as follows: As long as a state chooses to provide public education for some of its younger citizens, it must make it available for all children, and it must do so on an equal basis. Racially segregated education is not, and cannot be, equal, since it produces in black children a sense of inferiority and other types of psychological damage. In support of the latter point, the plaintiffs cited, and the Court accepted, the testimony of "modern authority," that is, social scientific evidence of the linkage between segregation and the development of negative self-concepts among black children.[17] In short, the cornerstone of the Brown ruling was the equal protection clause of the Fourteenth Amendment.[18]

It seems ironic that the applicability of the *Brown* ruling to the education of the handicapped was first noted by the counsel for the *Brown* defendants. John W. Davis (who, incidentally, was the Democratic presidential nominee in 1924) argued that if the Fourteenth Amendment was used to open up schools to blacks, there was no reason why it could not also serve as the basis for desegregation "on the ground of mental capacity."[19] Of course, this is precisely what happened over the last quarter-century. According to Thomas Gilhool,[20] echoes of the *Brown* decision can be found in two distinct types of special education litigation: those cases that argued for better standards for the identification and placement of handicapped children, and those that have centered on the right of the handicapped to public education. Several cases in the former group, including *Diana* v. *State Board of Education,* addressed the "stigmatizing" effects of special class placement and raised doubts that mildly retarded children could receive adequate, appropriate education in special classes.[21] Likewise, a number of right-to-education cases resulted in rulings that have extended the protection of the Fourteenth Amendment to include access to appropriate public education for retarded children[22] and, subsequently, for all handicapped children.[23] In these rulings, and in the legislation they helped bring about (such as P.L. 94-142), equal educational opportunity is not conceived primarily in terms of regular class placement. Rather, as has been previously stated, the basic obligation of states is to provide education that is *appropriate* to the needs of the individual child. This includes, among other things, the development of individualized education programs and placement in the least restrictive environment that is suited to the child's educational needs. Therefore, the existing legal precedent suggests that integration into regular classes is an option that can and should be used as the student's needs warrant.

Another aspect of the equal-educational entitlement argument is the view that integrated education constitutes a valuable socialization experience that will provide formerly segregated minorities with the attitudes and skills that underlie the ability to function successfully in society. Thus, it has been argued that daily contacts with white middle-class schoolmates will afford black pupils the chance to acquire the values, beliefs, and behavioral styles of the dominant social group within the United States.[24] Similarly, for the handicapped child, mainstreaming is presumed to represent an opportunity to acquire "naive psychology," that is, the tacit, universally shared assumptions about human behavior that are the bases for any social interactions.[25] Because some handicapped children (particularly the mentally retarded or the emotionally disturbed) who functioned exclusively in segregated settings may be deficient in these rudimentary social competencies, significant benefits would be derived from the placement of these children in mainstreamed classes, where teachers and peers could provide informal tutoring in routine interpersonal skills.[26]

These expectations for the transfer of values between different groups of students seem at first glance to be fairly realistic. After all, the classroom is an almost ideal locale for peer socialization. As Goslin has pointed out, friendship groups provide a setting in which children try out various social roles and behaviors, with little threat of serious punishment should the experiment go awry. It is through this gradual and relatively gentle process of playacting that children acquire an acquaintance with adult interaction patterns.[27] However, *intergroup* peer socialization—the transfer of values or norms across the boundaries of race or exceptionality—may be more problematic. In sociological terms, a school class constitutes a *membership group*, in that its participants belong to a certain category (e.g., Class 5-A, or Mr. Smith's homeroom). Membership groups are not necessarily *reference groups* (which serve as a source of social norms for participants), but only become such under certain circumstances.[28] Specifically, we would expect that unless some measure of integration is achieved in the classroom, the transfer of values from whites to blacks[29] and from normal pupils to the handicapped will occur rarely, if at all. According to Thomas Pettigrew, genuine integration (as opposed to mere desegregation) exists when equality and mutual acceptance occur between groups[30] (see chapter 4). What the issue boils down to is this: Intergroup peer socialization—an important objective of both mainstreaming and racial desegregation—requires a positive intergroup climate.

MAINSTREAMING AND TOLERANCE FOR DIVERSITY

As was noted in the discussion of racial relations in the classroom, there is a growing body of evidence to suggest that children's cross-racial interactions may be significantly influenced by normative climates and by organizational properties within the classroom (e.g., cooperative work groups). Nevertheless, these insights have only recently begun to emerge, and a considerable amount of additional work will be needed before we can claim to possess a really satisfactory understanding of the determinants of racial harmony in public schools.

The same must also be said about the mainstreamed classroom. While research has produced a handful of general conclusions about relationships between handicapped students and their nonhandicapped peers, these findings are not yet clear enough or consistent enough to be translated into specific policy guidelines for mainstreaming. What is known at the present time is that exceptional children typically occupy a low status in the informal social network of the school, and that integration into regular classes does not by itself enhance that status. Among the numerous causes for the handicapped pupil's social isolation, two general factors seem to be of greatest significance. First, exceptional children often differ from the majority on those properties that comprise the very heart of the student role. For example, disruptive behavior by educable mentally retarded pupils has been shown to promote peer rejection, while academic competence seems to have precisely the opposite effect.[31] Second, regardless of children's actual conduct or competence, there appears to be a stigma attached to exceptionality, and this may in itself generate some social distancing by the nonhandicapped. In a study comparing effects of "labeling" (the identification of individuals as handicapped) and those of actual contacts (between exceptional and normal peers), Cook and Wollersheim found the labeling process to be strongly associated with rejection (by normals), while subjects' prior experiences with the handicapped had little or no effect on rejection/acceptance.[32]

One generalization emerging from these and similar studies is this: While familiarity does not breed acceptance, similarity does. That is, the more unlike the majority (in terms of conduct, academic skill, or handicap) the exceptional student is or is perceived to be, the more likely it is that he or she will be rejected by normal classmates. Although this is certainly not a very hopeful conclusion, neither does it foreclose the possibility of amelioration. In order to enhance the status of handicapped students, or, more generally, improve the social climate of mainstreamed classrooms, special educators might look for guidance to the literature on racial relations. So far, there has been surprisingly little effort to apply interracial contact theory to mainstreaming. Yet the literature contains just enough examples of such attempts to attest to its potential usefulness. For instance, in much the same way that desegregation researchers have found that cooperative task structures promote relatively favorable relations between white and minority pupils, investigators have turned up evidence that cooperative activities may also induce acceptance of trainable mentally retarded children by their nonhandicapped peers.[33] Similarly, the teacher appears to play a critical role in both types of integration. While the evidence on this point is better established in the desegregation literature (see chapters 2 and 3), there are also some indications that the teacher's perceptions of handicapped pupils are reflected in the judgments of normal classmates.[34] Finally, demonstrations of mastery and competence seem to enhance the status of both newly integrated groups, as was demonstrated in Cohen's interracial expectations experiment,[35] and in at least one study of mainstreaming.[36] What seems to be important, then, is allocating tasks according to each child's level of ability, so that he or she will be able to demonstrate competence (to self and others) and thereby earn some measure of acceptance.[37]

Given the obvious parallels between these two forms of classroom integration, it would be tempting to surmise that mainstreaming might produce the same normative and behavioral outcomes that are believed to result from racial desegregation. In other words, the mainstreamed classroom could prove to be a useful vehicle for the socialization of functional tolerance. There are, however, several factors that cast doubt on this prospect. First, on those behaviors that matter most within the classroom—discipline and academic performance—the differences between exceptional and normal children are typically much greater than are any gaps between white and nonwhite pupils. Racial and ethnic distinctions are partly based on physical differences, which do not have a direct bearing on students' school performances, and on cultural patterns, which, in some cases, do. By contrast, the very nature of mental, emotional, or physical handicaps will set exceptional children apart from their classmates. That is, retardation entails a lower level of academic functioning, and emotional disturbances often pose serious problems for the child's adjustment to the school routine. And, with the stigma that is attached to handicapping conditions, exceptional pupils have an additional strike against them even before they have a chance to adjust to a mainstreamed setting. It is this combination of handicap and stigma that may make favorable relations between majority and minority more difficult to achieve in the mainstreamed classroom than in the racially desegregated school.

Another problem that may arise during mainstreaming derives from the special treatment of handicapped pupils, which is required by law, and the effects that such treatment may have on the socialization of nonhandicapped children. As has been discussed, pupils internalize universalistic norms through the teacher's even-handed application of rules and regulations to all members of the class. Yet it is difficult to see how universalistic standards can be reasonably applied in a mainstreamed class. According to P.L. 94-142, the education offered to handicapped children must be based on *individual* needs. As several writers have observed, there is considerable tension between two of the major goals of mainstreaming—individualized education and social integration, and the effort directed to the former may ultimately detract from the latter.[38] In concrete terms, it is reasonable to expect that nonhandicapped pupils (and their parents) will view exceptional children as competitors for the teacher's time and energies, and will come to resent them. Even if such resentment does not materialize, mainstreaming hardly represents an ideal condition for the transmission of the principles of equal treatment and impartiality. Nevertheless, the special opportunities for the socialization of the nonhandicapped afforded by mainstreaming should also be recognized. In particular, whatever decline schools may experience in their ability to transmit universalistic norms might be offset by opportunities for inculcating other desirable outcomes, notably a sense of responsibility and compassion. According to the narrative accounts of one classroom teacher, successful mainstreaming requires the active cooperation of nonhandicapped students, who must provide the assistance to their new classmates that teachers simply do not have time for.[39] It may be hoped, therefore, that when nonhandicapped children are directly and positively involved in the mainstreaming process, they will not view their exceptional classmates as competitors or nuisances, but rather as fellow human beings for whom they have some responsibility. The acquisition of such sentiments would be no small achievement. Indeed, it would be a far more desirable outcome than the neutral, detached orientation toward human diversity that has been discussed in this book.

In conclusion, the correspondence between mainstreaming and racial desegregation centers more on their common legal and historical foundations than on their implications for tolerance socialization. Whether the individualized treatment of special students impedes the development of universalistic norms, or fosters a spirit of peer responsibility and compassion, is one important issue that remains to be determined.

6

Multicultural Education

In certain respects, multiculturalism is not a new issue for American education. Schools have always dealt with students from diverse subcultures, and have traditionally included at least some multicultural content and themes within the formal curriculum. What is different about the current effort is the explicit emphasis placed on children's cultural backgrounds as a determinant of both school performances and long-term values and behaviors. Unlike the more traditional approaches, multiculturalism requires schools to openly acknowledge the value of human variation and to make it a central consideration in the formulation of curricular, instructional, and management policies. Our discussion of this topic will focus on three major issues: first, the background and purposes of multicultural education; second, its consequences for students; and third, its possible effects on society at large. In so doing, we will be especially interested in the possible ramifications of the new multiculturalism for intergroup relations in the school and elsewhere.

ORIGINS AND OBJECTIVES

Much has been said of the "ethnic renaissance" currently underway in the United States.[1] For a variety of reasons,

Americans are placing renewed importance on their ancestral heritage, especially as it pertains to racial and ethnic identities. As was discussed in chapter 1, the new ethnicity serves a variety of functions, including personal affiliation and the attainment of political and economic rewards. To a considerable degree, this movement is an outgrowth of the black-led civil rights campaign of the 1950s and 1960s. As heightened awareness and cohesive organization among blacks resulted in substantial social and political reforms, so other groups, including Hispanics, Native Americans, and some white ethnics, have applied similar strategies in pursuit of their own claims and interests. Finally, nonethnic groups, such as women, the handicapped, the elderly, and homosexuals, have also adopted the principles of collective solidarity, with the result that the concept of social or cultural diversity now has a much broader meaning within American life than at any point in recent history. Manifestations of this tendency can be found almost everywhere. Its symbolic aspects are perhaps best reflected in the nationality days and cultural festivals held in many metropolitan areas, in the growing popularity of ethnic social and cultural associations, and in the increased representation of minority groups in the popular media. The economic and political objectives of subgroup affiliation are most conspicuously evidenced in the affirmative-action policies of government, universities, and private industry.

The movement toward pluralism within the larger society is also illustrated in the burgeoning popularity of multicultural education. However, the most direct influence on multiculturalism in the schools has been government policy, particularly at the federal level. Beginning in the mid-1960s, Congress passed a series of laws authorizing school programs intended to improve the educational prospects of students from minority backgrounds. By 1975, more than $500 million was being appropriated annually for bilingual education, education of Native Americans, programs for children of migratory farm workers, desegregation assistance, and ethnic studies.[2] As originally developed, the federal strategy centered on efforts to facilitate the racial desegregation of schools. For instance, the 1964 Civil Rights Act authorized termination of funding to any district not in compliance with federal desegregation policy. Eight years later, the Emergency School Aid Act provided for a variety of activities, including teacher and counselor training and curriculum development, intended to encourage schools to serve the needs of racially diverse student bodies. Also in 1972, Title VII of the Elementary and Secondary Education Act provided grants for bilingual programs, ranging from early childhood to adult education. While all of these laws have had a clear impact on the growth of multicultural programs, it was only in the Ethnic Heritage Studies Act (Title IX of the Elementary and Secondary Education Act) of 1972 that Congress explicitly advocated the study of minority subcultures by all students.[3] According to the principal author of this legislation, schools should work toward the creation of a "new pluralism" through the study of a "great American resource: ethnicity and cultural diversity."[4] In addition to federal laws, certain rulings by federal courts have spurred the growth of multicultural education. Of particular importance is the U.S. Supreme Court's *Lau* v. *Nichols* decision,[5] which required bilingual instruction for Chinese-speaking students in San Francisco. By 1980, the U.S. Department of Education expanded the *Lau* ruling by mandating bilingual education for all pupils whose primary language is other than English. (This policy has since been rescinded under the Reagan administration.)

Not all of the push for multiculturalism, however, has originated with the federal government. As of 1975, all but a few state departments of education were requiring some form of multiculturalism in the schools or were providing technical assistance or resources for bilingual and ethnic studies programs.[6] Colleges and universities, particularly those engaged in teacher preparation, were another important source of support. In fact, the clearest and most influential elaboration of the purposes of multicultural education was that issued by the American Association of Colleges for Teacher Education (AACTE). In its statement, AACTE suggested that the ultimate goal of multicultural education is nothing less than the creation and maintenance of a genuinely tolerant, pluralistic society:

> The positive elements of a culturally pluralistic society will be realized only if there is a healthy interaction among the diverse groups which comprise the nation's citizenry. Such interaction enables all to share in the richness of America's multicultural heritage. Such interaction provides a means for coping with the intercultural tensions that are natural and cannot be avoided in a growing, dynamic society. To accept cultural pluralism is to recognize that no group lives in a vacuum—that each group exists as part of an interrelated whole.[7]

To achieve this end, AACTE identified four preferred approaches to multicultural education:

1. the teaching of values which support cultural diversity and individual uniqueness;
2. the encouragement of the qualitative expansion of existing ethnic cultures and their incorporation into the mainstream of American socioeconomic and political life;
3. the support of explorations in alternative and emerging life styles;
4. the encouragement of multiculturalism, multilingualism, and multidialectism.[8]

One key component of the new programs is the education (or re-education) of teachers for multiculturalism. According to one commentator, teacher training in this field should seek to produce a variety of outcomes, including knowledge of the principles of cultural pluralism, knowledge of appropriate multicultural resources, favorable attitudes toward racial and ethnic diversity, and skill and sensitivity in intercultural communication and instruction.[9] Teachers, in other words, are expected to overcome whatever biases they may have, to become familiar with the sociocultural factors that influence students' school performance, and to serve as models for appropriate intergroup behavior. Nevertheless, the success or failure of multicultural education will ultimately depend on the students themselves. Although multicultural programs address a variety of objectives, it is evident from the wording of the various master plans that their principal goal is racial and ethnic tolerance.

OUTCOMES FOR STUDENTS AND SCHOOLS

As was discussed in chapter 3, tolerance for diversity can be thought of as taking two forms. *Symbolic tolerance* describes favorable attitudes toward some abstract or hypothetical representation of political or ethnic diversity, such as support for the principles of civil liberties or racial equality. *Functional tolerance* is the condition in which members of diverse groups are willing and able to work together in the pursuit of shared goals. Whereas symbolic tolerance has been a traditional objective of public education, we have seen that the schools may be more successful in fostering functional expressions of intergroup toleration. Multicultural education, it seems fair to say, aims at both types of outcomes. That is, it seeks to induce changes in students' attitudes and in their behaviors.

In the past, direct efforts to reduce or eliminate authoritarianism and prejudice among students have not been notably successful, apparently because standard instructional approaches are geared more toward transmission of knowledge than toward modification of attitudes. What appears to be required instead is the opportunity for students to become personally engaged in these matters. Thus, strong identification with a positive role model, such as the teacher, and participation in simulations and role playing have been found to induce attitudinal change.[10] In this respect, multiculturalism would seem to have a reasonably good chance for success. As noted previously, strong emphasis is placed on the teacher's role as a model of desirable intergroup attitudes and behaviors. Although multicultural programs vary greatly in specific procedures, the emphasis on affect and values that is generally a part of such courses might well enhance their effectiveness in fostering symbolic tolerance. In addition, the new courses have considerable potential for promoting functional tolerance. According to interracial contact theory, institutions facilitate cooperative interactions between groups by providing strong, overt support for racial and ethnic harmony and by attempting to ensure equality of status for all groups.[11] Both conditions appear to be adequately addressed in the overall framework of multicultural education. Institutional supports take the form of the positive roles played by teachers, counselors, and administrators. Status equalization is approached through teachers' even-handed treatment of all students, and through instructional emphasis on both the contributions of minority groups to American life and the inherent value and desirability of cultural diversity. Also, as schools adapt their academic and social routines to the needs of minority pupils, those students may feel more comfortable within, and less alienated from, the school milieu.

Having presented a decidedly optimistic forecast so far, we should also consider some of the possible limitations and drawbacks of multiculturalism. First, it seems quite evident that these new programs are best suited for use in multiracial, multiethnic schools. Students in all-white or all-minority classrooms have little opportunity for the sustained interactions that are the essence of functional tolerance. Moreover, lectures on the value of cultural pluralism might seem to be hollow and even hypocritical if a school's enrollment is limited to members of a single group. Second, the success of such programs will depend heavily on educators' wholehearted commitment to the principles and purposes of multicultural education, and on their skill in carrying out instructional and management activities. Undoubtedly, some teachers will be much less favorably disposed toward multicultural education than will others, and in such cases it is doubtful that the desired outcomes can be achieved. To be sure, teachers and principals have in the past carried out policies, such as racial desegregation or mainstreaming, that they may not have favored. Multiculturalism, however, entails a higher level of personal commitment. as it asks educators not only to teach, but also to model attitudes and values.

Finally, there is an even more basic concern that attends the wholesale implementation of multicultural programs. Stated simply, the possibility exists that a sustained emphasis on race and ethnicity will upset the relatively fragile intergroup climate that now characterizes many desegregated schools in the United States. As has been amply documented in recent ethnographic research, teachers and students generally seem to feel that the less said about racial matters, the better. For instance, several observers have emphasized the important part played by color-blind policies within the formal organization of desegregated schools and classrooms.[12] Likewise, informal activities are approached on the basis of "natural progression," that is, the assumption that students will work out a reasonable pattern of intergroup relations for themselves.[13] In such situations, a deliberate emphasis on racial and ethnic concerns may backfire by calling attention to factors that divide students or by uncovering latent tensions. Conceivably, the celebration of certain subcultures or the adaptation of classroom practices to accommodate the special needs of some pupils may be interpreted by other students as favoritism. The counterargument is, of course, that multiculturalism is not divisive, and that through the schools' redressing the long-standing neglect of cultural diversity within curricular and instructional policies, students will become more accepting of those social and cultural differences that had previously set them apart.[14]

OUTCOMES FOR SOCIETY

In order to forecast the long-term consequences of multicultural education for intergroup relations in American life, we must first understand the loosely formulated social philosophy in which this movement is rooted, namely, cultural pluralism. As described by Tesconi, cultural pluralism maintains that

> any human society is best served by maximizing the distinctiveness of different tastes and values, not only in the political and economic realms, but in the religious, ethnic, racial, [and] indeed cultural realms as well. As a descriptive account of

America, then, cultural pluralism holds that this nation is a complex interlocking of ethnic and other groups whose members pursue their diverse interests through the medium of private associations, which in turn are coordinated, negotiated, encouraged, and guided by a federal system of representative democracy.[15]

In the United States at least, cultural pluralism has been closely linked to democratic theory. According to one of its earliest proponents, "cultural pluralism is possible only in a democratic society," because no other form of government permits the melding of individual interests into the "fellowship(s) of freedom and cooperation" that are the bases of pluralism.[16] More recently, however, effort has been made to separate the concepts of cultural pluralism and political democracy. Van den Berghe, for instance, suggests that culturally pluralist nations are partly held together by political coercion, and that "there is no necessary or universal association of pluralism with either democracy or tyranny."[17] Nevertheless, the prevailing view appears to be that pluralism not only springs from democracy, but also helps to preserve it. One way in which it does so is by making available a wide range of values, ideas, and beliefs. Thus, the pluralist philosophy holds that

> any society is richer if it will allow a thousand flowers to blossom. The assumption is that no man's culture or way of life is so rich that it may not be further enriched by contact with other points of view. The conviction is that diversity is enriching because no man has a monopoly on the truth about the good life.[18]

Pluralism is also thought to improve the individual's relationship with the surrounding social system. It has been said that modern societies are characterized by a pervasive sense of malaise or alienation, stemming from the fast pace of industrialization, the eradication of traditional values and institutions, and an overpowering feeling of rootlessness and meaninglessness.[19] Under such circumstances, affiliation with one's ethnic or racial group provides individuals with a specialized status, and reduces tendencies toward alienation.[20] Finally, genuine cultural pluralism may have important political benefits, insofar as the representation of organized racial, ethnic, and religious interests would seem to contribute to the vitality of democratic values. Clearly, it was not until blacks began to organize and to flex their collective political muscle that the federal government began to make any serious effort to abolish racial segregation in housing, employment, education, and elsewhere.

The overall theory of cultural pluralism, therefore, seeks to achieve a series of goals that very few people are likely to oppose. In addition, multicultural education addresses other objectives that seem equally desirable, such as the promotion of socioeconomic mobility among minority youngsters. This goal derives from the belief that American education has traditionally been based on a very narrow cultural framework (that of the white Anglo-Saxon) and, as a result, has assigned minority students to a marginal status in the schools. If the schools are opened to the needs, interests, and concerns of subcultural groups, minority pupils will succeed on an approximately equal basis with other students. Hence, multicultural education is viewed as a stepping-stone to social and economic equality.[21]

Despite these obviously appealing goals and objectives, multicultural education, together with the supporting philosophy of cultural pluralism, has in recent years been roundly criticized. In very broad terms, the basic objection centers on the belief that multiculturalism is inherently divisive and will contribute to the disintegration of American society. For purposes of clarity and convenience, these objections will be reviewed in two parts. The first point is that multicultural education will only exacerbate the presently marginal status of racial minorities, while the second holds that under the current state of intergroup relations in this society, increased emphasis on subcultural distinctiveness will strain existing tensions to the breaking point.

Multiculturalism, Mobility, and Racial Relations

One central premise of pluralist theory is that the United States is fundamentally a culturally heterogeneous society. The most distinctive subcultures are thought to exist among racial and, to a lesser extent, ethnic minorities. Thus, blacks, Hispanics, Native Americans, Asians, and some white immigrant groups are said to hold values and ways of life that are at odds with, or at least clearly distinguishable from, the American cultural mainstream.[22] Recently, however, it has been argued that whatever subcultural differences exist within the American population are essentially trivial. According to Ryan, "specific differences that might be identified as signs of separate cultural identity are relatively insignificant within the general unity of American life; they are cultural commas and semicolons in the paragraphs and pages of American life."[23]

Some observers think that ethnic groups may have deliberately exaggerated their own distinctiveness in hopes of attaining psychological satisfaction or economic rewards. Parsons, for instance, suggests that ethnic identification has a largely symbolic value in that it allows the individual to function freely within the social mainstream while carving out a more personalized status.[24] Greeley makes the same point specifically with respect to white ethnic groups: "Ethnicity is not a way of looking back to the old world. Most of the immigrants were only too happy to get the hell out of it. Ethnicity is rather a way of being American . . . the last thing in the world that the new ethnic upper-middle class wants is to define itself out of the common American culture."[25]

This is not to suggest that the United States has achieved complete integration. On the contrary, structural pluralism—the existence of parallel institutions that perform the same functions for different groups—appears to be much more pervasive than cultural pluralism. Gordon argues that the cultural assimilation of minorities almost invariably precedes their integration into the institutional mainstream of society.[26] Turn-of-the-century immigrants, for example, were generally quick to adopt English as their primary language, yet maintained strong and active ties to the churches or synagogues, social and fraternal organizations, and neighborhoods of their nationality groups. Likewise, van den Berghe suggests that while some "cultural drift" has occurred between blacks and whites, the far-reaching racial caste system of the United States is most appropriately described in terms of structural pluralism.[27]

The point therefore is that, in contrast with pluralist theory, some current observers believe that the gaps between racial and ethnic groups have not been fundamentally cultural in nature. If this is true, the schools could perhaps best serve the interests of minority students not by reinforcing minor subcultural variations, but by transmitting the academic and social skills required to enter the socioeconomic mainstream. As we have already seen, upward mobility *is* a goal of multicultural education, in that pluralists hope to make American society in general more receptive to its minority cultures, and the schools in particular more responsive to the needs of minority students. Nevertheless, the case has sometimes been made that ethnic studies courses and other exercises in educational pluralism might actually limit minority children's chances for socioeconomic mobility.

In one sense, it seems naive to assume that multicultural school programs will effect any meaningful change in society. According to numerous social critics, the racial caste and social class systems that exist in the United States are so well entrenched as to be beyond the reach of such limited attempts at reform as multicultural education.[28] Since American society is unlikely to have changed substantially by the time the alumni of today's ethnic studies courses graduate, it seems pointless, even cruel, to some observers to provide children with skills and orientations for a pluralistic society that does not and will not exist. Thus, multicultural education is sometimes seen as detracting from the real needs of minority students.[29] From this vantage point, multiculturalism is a product of well-meaning dreamers, and is ultimately injurious to the interests of minorities. In an even harsher appraisal, Patterson asserts that pluralism is a sophisticated device for furthering the isolation of blacks, and thus functions as a tool of "the most reactionary and vicious elements of society."[30]

In pursuing its goal of social and economic equality, multicultural education also aims at the improvement of racial and ethnic relations in the United States. Relationships based on the cultural, economic, and political dominance of one group, and the subjugation of others, are clearly not what pluralists have in mind when they speak of the "healthy interactions among diverse groups" that provide "a means for coping with . . . intercultural tensions."[31] And, of course, multiculturalism also seeks to foster racial and ethnic tolerance more directly, by inducing changes in the knowledge, attitudes, and behaviors of students.

Criticism of multiculturalism, on the other hand, often suggests that heightened awareness of racial or ethnic identification is divisive. In the words of R.P. Wolff, "out-group hostility is the natural accompaniment of in-group loyalty. The more warmly a man says "'we,' the more coldly will he say 'they.'"[32] From this perspective, pluralism contains the seeds of separatism, and therefore poses problems for any society that is already characterized by some degree of racial and ethnic fragmentation. Pratte warns that the new emphasis on subcultural diversity may awaken the simmering racial and ethnic tensions that lie not very far below the surface of American life.[33]

A related concern is that the pursuit of narrow group interests will detract from attainment of the overall welfare. Traditionally, the group has functioned as an intermediary between the society and the individual, and builds loyalties to the national system as it builds loyalties to itself.[34] Hence, basic societal needs, such as economic productivity and national security, are seen as transcending parochial group interests, and society is regarded as more than merely the sum of its constituent subgroups. A perfectly pluralistic society, however, is "an aggregate of human communities rather than itself a human community," and therefore provides "no mechanism for the discovery and expression of the common good."[35]

In the United States, one factor that has contributed to the balance of parochial and general interests has been the willingness and ability of most Americans to limit the importance of their own subgroup affiliations. Because each one of us plays so many roles, and thus has a variety of interests and loyalties, we typically cannot afford to allow any one single facet of our background or identity to override all others. Accordingly, most individuals' social and political behaviors are shaped by some combination of diverse loyalties, ties, and interests.[36] A particularly vivid example of these cross-pressures can be found in the current experiences of many middle-class blacks. Given the racial history of the United States, it would not be suprising if blacks chose to see themselves as a group essentially apart from the rest of society and placed far greater emphasis on their racial identification than on any other status or role. However, at least one survey has found that most blacks regard themselves as "equally black and American."[37] Among the factors that have apparently worked against the emergence of a widespread separatist orientation is the recent expansion of educational and occupational opportunities for blacks to the extent that some observers think that race per se is now of much less significance than social class in determining the life chances of black Americans.[38] Upper-middle-class blacks in particular would seem to be caught between two broad sets of interests. On the one hand, many of these individuals support political, social, and economic reform as a means for improving the prospects of less-advantaged members of their racial group. At the same time, however, some have developed strong financial and professional interests that might be better served by more conservative policies.[39] Of course, not only blacks but most Americans are cross-pressured in this way, and it is precisely this delicate balancing of interests that critics of pluralism fear will be threatened if individuals are encouraged to place all of their eggs, so to speak, in the single basket of race or ethnicity. As Wolff has suggested, the genius of American politics is its spirit of compromise.[40] Should racial or ethnic concerns come to constitute the entirety of Americans' interests, and, in effect, become nonnegotiable, compromise will be unlikely or even impossible.

CONCLUSION

In attempting to summarize some of the arguments for and against multicultural education, there is a danger of over-generalization. As Banks and others have noted, multicul-turalism is actually a blanket term that includes a wide array of distinct curricula and policies such as bilingualism, ethnic studies (which primarily seek to impart information about specific groups), multiethnic education (which pertains to the total school experiences of students from "victimized" racial and ethnic groups), and course work in the overall phenomenon of cultural pluralism.[41] Accordingly, each of these different types of multicultural education can be expected to have different effects on students.

In view of the delicate state of racial and ethnic relations in American schools (and in American life in general), the most desirable types of multicultural programs would seem to be those that aim at specific skills, rather than broad affective outcomes. Included among these skill programs are bilingual instruction for pupils with minimal competence in English, in-service courses intended to sensitize teachers to the academic needs of minority students, and utilization of some racial and ethnic themes and concerns within traditional curricula. Somewhat more problematic are courses in cultural pluralism itself, and ethnic studies courses emphasizing group distinctiveness. The objection to courses that celebrate diversity for its own sake stems partly from the conviction that most of these efforts will prove fruitless or even counterproductive. As research has consistently demonstrated, direct instruction is not an effective vehicle for changing students' racial or ethnic attitudes. Traditionally successful techniques—those requiring a very high degree of emotional involvement—may be too risky for widespread use, in that they could upset the delicate intergroup climates found in many desegregated schools. Likewise, courses that stress the uniqueness or distinctiveness of racial or ethnic groups rather than their commonalities and their contributions to the general good run contrary to the unwritten policies of color-blindness and natural progression that are the foundations of functional tolerance in schools and elsewhere.

It should be evident that the goals of multicultural education represent only a small part of the school's overall socialization mission. While some amount of multiculturalism seems desirable, we may consider Glazer's suggestion that the primary thrust of public education should be directed to the transmission of the common culture. Thus, the preferred place of cultural pluralism within public education is as a "supplement to the emerging common interests and common ideals that bind all groups in the society; it does not, and should not, describe the whole" (of socialization within the school).[42] This point is sometimes lost among pluralist educators, who seem to assume that the core culture will inevitably assert itself.

Although a substantial degree of culture conformity does exist within the national population, as Gordon, van den Berghe, and others have suggested, it cannot be assumed that the integration of American society has been accomplished in any final form. For one thing, native-born minorities, including blacks and Native Americans, continue to experience dramatic inequities in housing, income, and other areas. In addition, the United States is currently receiving hundreds of thousands of new immigrants every year. With the changes in federal immigration policy in 1965, the great majority of new arrivals are now coming from Third World areas such as Indochina and Latin America that had been effectively excluded under the previous system. Lacking ties to earlier generations of immigrants, the recent arrivals often cluster in small, tightly knit, and homogeneous enclaves and have, in some instances, remained relatively isolated from outsiders.[43] If the younger members of these groups are to be given a reasonable chance for meaningful participation within the institutional mainstream, it will very likely be public education that provides much of that opportunity. Accordingly, the major contribution of the schools in the years ahead will not be reinforcement of students' distinctive subcultural patterns, but rather the transmission of the values, skills, and behaviors that are most characteristic of American society as a whole.

7

Education and Tolerance in the 1980s

At the outset of the 1980s, American public opinion and social policy appeared to be shifting away from the spirit and climate of the previous few decades. Whereas much of the post–World War II era had been characterized by the steadily increasing size and scope of public agencies and by a widespread movement toward social reform, the tide has more recently turned in the direction of fiscal and governmental restraint. Perhaps the most conspicious manifestation of this trend was the election of a conservative Republican president in 1980, and the substantial gains registered by conservatives in both houses of Congress in that same year.

While the depth and permanence of this trend remain uncertain, there is little doubt that public education will be among those institutions immediately and significantly affected. On assuming office, President Reagan called for across-the-board reductions in educational expenditures amounting to 25 percent of the previous budgetary proposals, and also began to carry out his campaign pledge of a less active federal role in public education. At the same time, there has been ample evidence of general dissatisfaction with both the process and products of public schooling. As test scores have continued to decline, the demand has increased for various forms of educational accountability. In addition to its perceived academic deficiencies, public education was being charged with moral and disciplinary laxity. For these and other reasons, private schools, particularly those affiliated with conservative religious denominations, have begun to show new strength in enrollments. Another target of the critics was the social programs implemented in the schools during the previous fifteen years. In some areas, efforts to achieve racial desegregation were being curtailed or eliminated. Ironically, the rollback in these programs was occurring at a time when intergroup tensions were once again on the rise. Extremist groups, such as the Ku Klux Klan, were back in the news and there appeared to be an increased incidence of assaults on members of minority groups.

The changing national mood may have important implications for the socialization of tolerance. Although the actual effects of our shifting national priorities will not be known for several years, some impact is inevitable, in that many of the policies and programs that pertain directly to the socialization of tolerance (see chapters 3, 5, and 6) are largely the products of a public and, especially, of a federal commitment to equal opportunity and cultural pluralism that may be rapidly disappearing.

THE REDUCED ROLE OF GOVERNMENT

The intentions of the Reagan administration in the field of education may be judged on the basis of promises made in the 1980 campaign and actions taken on assumption of office.[1] Nearly all of these point to a sharply reduced federal role in both higher education and in the public schools. Consider the following:

1. One of the first acts of Secretary of Education Terrell H. Bell was to rescind a major provision of the previous admin-

istration's bilingual program—specifically, the requirement that full instructional programs be offered in any native language spoken by at least twenty-five students in any one district.

2. At about the same time, Mr. Bell announced that the Department of Justice would introduce no new suits seeking the racial desegregation of public schools, and that the federal government would proceed less vigorously with efforts to promote racial balance within college and university systems in South Carolina, Delaware, Texas, Virginia, and several other states.

3. On several occasions, Mr. Reagan has announced support in principle for a constitutional amendment against the use of busing for school desegregation.

4. In May 1982, Mr. Reagan declared his intention to seek legislation that would provide tax credits to parents paying tuition for their children's education in nonpublic schools.

5. With the concurrence of Congress, the Reagan administration has sharply reduced the federal government's role in financing higher education. While the principal victims of the cutbacks in the federally guaranteed loan program were students from middle-income families, the so-called Pell grants, which provide aid to lower-income students, were also reduced by some $80 million in 1981–1982, with further cuts expected in subsequent years.

In addition to reducing its aid to students, the administration has lowered its direct allocations to public schools, to colleges and universities, and to supporting government agencies. While the proposed cuts range across many program areas, they appear to be particularly concentrated among social, as opposed to essentially academic, policies, including the school lunch program for low-income students and the National Science Foundation's effort to recruit women and minorities into scientific careers. Also affected was the National Institute of Education, which had previously provided much of the research base for desegregation, mainstreaming, and multiculturalism.

Another threat to the schools' social programs is the likelihood that in a period of reduced revenues, states and school districts will direct funds away from social policies toward higher-priority academic programs. Consider, for example, the growing popularity of Minimum Competency Testing (MCT), which, as of 1980, was required in thirty-three states.[2] Although the essence of competency testing is simply a heightened instructional emphasis on those basic academic skills that are already included in nearly every high school curriculum, MCT programs can be quite costly, especially when extensive remediation of low-achieving students is called for. In most states, remediation will be funded from local revenues rather than from supplementary allocations from the state. Since competency testing typically enjoys widespread support from both political leaders and the public at large, it will probably compete successfully with less academically oriented programs for the revenues that remain available to public education after the federal and state budget cuts. This is all the more likely to occur as the Reagan administration carries out its pledge to channel much federal funding through block grants, which may be expended on programs selected by the states and local districts, rather than through categorical grants, which are targeted to specific areas and have been a major vehicle for supporting the schools' social programs.

Taken together, these new budgetary and policy priorities would seem to forecast a bleak future for tolerance socialization efforts in public education. If the schools are required to emphasize their academic function at the expense of other types of citizenship training, students may be less prepared to participate in the complex interpersonal and intergroup relationships that are an important part of American social life. However, there are also at least a few grounds for cautious optimism. First, the schools' effectiveness in shaping social outcomes may be relatively impervious to short-term fluctuations in the political and economic climate. Recall, for example, that norms of fairness and color-blindness are believed to be transmitted indirectly, through the ordinary routines of the classroom, rather than through deliberate attempts to achieve this end. Indeed, discussions in previous chapters have expressed concern that some such direct efforts might backfire. Some varieties of multicultural education, as well as mainstreaming of the handicapped, seem to run particularly high risks of counterproductivity. If either or both of these programs should be substantially curtailed in the near future, what will be lost is not the certainty of increased tolerance for diversity, but the possibility of determining the effectiveness of these programs.

Also, it should be recognized that racial desegregation is an accomplished fact throughout much of American public education, and barring certain extreme developments (which will be discussed shortly), will continue as such. Furthermore, the Reagan administration's unwillingness to pursue challenges to de facto segregation in no way prevents private groups from doing so. The federal government, in fact, was a relatively late entrant into the long battle to eliminate racial dualism in the schools. It has more typically been organizations such as the National Association for the Advancement of Colored People (NAACP) that have carried the burden of achieving equal educational opportunities for blacks and other minorities. Although extensive and prolonged legal efforts may strain the resources of private groups, it is noteworthy that both revenues and memberships in NAACP, Americans for Democratic Action, and other defenders of civil rights and civil liberties are said to have increased substantially in the immediate aftermath of the 1980 elections.

While the withdrawal of the executive branch need not spell the end of the school integration effort, there are certain efforts currently afoot in Congress that enjoy the support of the Reagan administration and that most definitely raise the prospect of a national retreat from the principle and practice of school desegregation. The first of these is the proposed constitutional amendment against the use of school busing to achieve racial balance. Although there is little likelihood that this amendment will be approved by Congress or ratified by the requisite thirty-eight state legislatures at any time in the near future, a more immediate threat to school desegregation efforts exists in the form of a bill that would place a five-mile limit on the distance that any child may be bused for purposes of desegregation. Given the pervasiveness of racial discrimination in housing, enactment of this bill would place many American schools in a condition of racial imbalance not seen in the last quarter-century. Finally, the maintenance of social diversity in school enrollments might also be jeopardized by a bill that provides tax credits of up to $500 for parents whose children are enrolled in private schools. While this bill has been voted down in previous sessions, it may now benefit from the active support of the Reagan administration. Since the proposed legislation would effectively subsidize private education, it might very well result in significant enrollment declines in the public schools. Furthermore, such subsidies might be most attractive to middle-income parents, insofar as private school tuitions would generally remain beyond the reach of lower-income families. Under these circumstances, it would not be unreasonable to predict that public education would come to be perceived as the province of low-income and minority students, while private schools would continue and even expand their present role as institutions serving an overwhelmingly white, middle- to upper-middle class clientele.

The substantial support in Congress for the tuition tax credit bill is based partly on the long-held desire of the newly dominant conservatives to turn back to the private sector some of the functions that have been assumed by government. However, it is also indicative of another trend much in evidence at the outset of the 1980s—the demand for religious instruction and observance in the schools. This movement has taken a variety of forms and poses a significant challenge to certain traditions of American education.

RELIGION AND THE SCHOOLS

On April 7, 1981, the National Center for Educational Statistics released a draft version of a report entitled *Public and Private*

Schools. The report's principal author was Professor James Coleman of the University of Chicago, a well-known sociologist who was also primarily responsible for the massive study of equality of educational opportunity commissioned by Congress in 1964.[3] As part of an ongoing study of public and private education in the United States, the new Coleman report was intended to provide answers to a host of critical policy questions, including the relative effectiveness of public and private schools in producing various academic, social, and psychological outcomes. In brief, the report concluded that private schools were more successful in achieving desired cognitive outcomes, provided safer and more disciplined environments, and, at least in the case of the Catholic schools (which comprised about two-thirds of the private sector sample), more closely approached the "common school ideal of American education" than did the public schools.[4]

Much of the initial reaction to the Coleman study was strongly critical. Sparked in part perhaps by the concern that the report's results would be used for political purposes (specifically, to generate support for the pending tuition tax credit bill), critics charged that the study was badly flawed in almost all respects, including sampling, analysis, and interpretation.[5] Nevertheless, Coleman's conclusions appeared to be entirely consistent with the prevailing perception of the contemporary status of public and private education in the United States. For instance, shortly after Coleman's findings were released, a national newsmagazine ran a special report entitled "Why Public Schools Are Flunking," which documented the various problems of public education and the reasons for the increasing attractiveness of private schools.[6]

The debate over the relative merits of public and private schools is not a new one. The two forms of education have sometimes been thought of as complementary, and at other times as mutually opposed. Throughout much of the post–World War II era, private schools appeared to be in decline. Between 1966 and 1974, for example, the proportion of all elementary school students accounted for by the private sector dropped from 14.3 percent to 10.5.[7] Recently however, non-public schools have rebounded, with small but consistent gains in their proportion of total enrollment.[8] The most common explanations for the resurgence of private schools is the perceived weakness of public education, which is seen as plagued by drug abuse, violence, vandalism, and racial tension among students, and by apathy, incompetence, and "burnout" among teachers.[9] Thus, in accordance with the Coleman report, the private school is often seen as a safer, more productive environment than its public counterpart.

There is another factor that may be even more important in explaining the current appeal of private education. Throughout their history, most nonpublic schools have had a strong religious orientation. Today, more than three-quarters of all private schools in the United States are church affiliated.[10] By far the most numerous of these are Roman Catholic parochial schools. However, the fastest growing element of private education is those schools sponsored by Protestant denominations. Particularly in the South, these institutions usually take the form of "Christian academies," which reflect the fundamentalist orientations of their sponsoring churches.[11] In many parochial schools, Catholic, fundamentalist, and otherwise, religion is included within the school routine through prayers and other observances, through religious instruction, and through the infusion of religious themes into otherwise secular subject content.

To some extent, the enduring popularity of parochial schools can be attributed to factors other than religion per se. For example, Steinberg has suggested that Catholic schools have promoted "ethnic as well as religious purposes," serving as repositories of Irish, Italian, Polish, and other subcultures.[12] Likewise, it is probably not coincidental that the growth of Christian academies did not take place until large-scale desegregation efforts were initiated in the public schools of the South. And, as previously indicated, parochial and other private schools are often thought to offer more stable environments than their public counterparts. Nevertheless, the desire of many parents to include a strong religious orientation within their children's education should not be underestimated. Indeed, the demand for nonsecular education is not limited to the clientele of private schools. Despite a string of federal and state court rulings that explicitly prohibit religious observance or instruction in the public schools, various forms of "nondenominational" observance routinely occur. Schools in Ohio and Kentucky, for example, have defied court orders by posting the Ten Commandments on bulletin boards and by conducting team prayers before athletic contests. Recently, President Reagan and several influential members of Congress have announced their support of a constitutional amendment that would permit "voluntary" prayer in public schools.

In addition, there is considerable sentiment that the "creationist" account of the origins of the human race should be taught alongside evolutionary theory within school science classes. In 1981, the governors of Arkansas and Louisiana signed bills requiring such instruction. Although the Arkansas law has already been ruled unconstitutional, creationists in other states are still seeking to have courts require similar programs, and are likely to continue to do so, especially in view of President Reagan's expressed support for such a policy. Finally, public school textbooks and curriculum materials are being closely scrutinized in some areas by committees affiliated with fundamentalist groups that attempt to exclude materials not sufficiently in line with their own beliefs.

Each of these cases illustrates the current effort to desecularize American education. Proponents of this movement appear to believe that public schools overreacted to the Supreme Court's rulings on church-state separation in the 1960s not only by expunging all traces of religion but also by emphasizing a social and moral outlook that is inconsistent with the beliefs of many students and their parents. In the eyes of the fundamentalists, this approach is not morally neutral or value-free, but instead embodies secular, humanistic values that are antithetical to religion, patriotism, and traditional family life. Thus, to counteract the influence of an alien value system, opponents of "secular humanism" have sought to reintroduce religious rites and instruction within public education or have created their own schools.

The intention here is not to offer a sweeping criticism of the overall antisecularist position. Indeed, certain points seem to have considerable merit, including the claim that the secular emphasis of public school instruction is not value-free, and in fact runs contrary to the cherished beliefs of many Americans. Likewise, the case for tuition tax credits may be strengthened by the fact that public subsidies of private schools are readily available in many other multiethnic, democratic nations. Rather, our interest centers on the possible implications of this movement for the socialization of tolerance in American schools, and in this respect, the consequences of any wholesale desecularization of American education are likely to be over-whelmingly negative. With respect to religious observance in public schools, federal courts have on numerous occasions ruled that such practices represent a clear violation of the First Amendment, especially as they infringe on the rights of religious minorities and nonbelievers.[13] From the perspective of this book, the reintroduction of religion into the classroom would provide yet another basis for divisiveness and contention among students, thereby hampering the school's efforts to transmit a common culture and promote tolerance. For those who insist on a religious orientation in the education of their children, the appropriate alternative is a parochial school. Yet, as has already been argued, any mass movement away from public schools might result in increased segregation. As is ac-knowledged by Professor Coleman, "Private schools are divisive along religious lines, segregating different religious groups into different schools."[14] In addition, private schools presently en-roll much smaller proportions of black students than do the public schools. Coleman's claim that a tuition tax credit bill would increase minority enrollments in private schools has been criticized as being unsupported and even contradicted by his data,[15] and Coleman has subsequently backed off somewhat from this position.[16]

To summarize, it has been argued that the desecularization of public schools would constitute a violation of students' civil liberties and would increase tensions and divisiveness. Large-scale abandonment of public education for private schools would very probably increase racial, religious, and socio-economic segregation. In short, the religion-in-the-schools movement, if successful, could undermine the effectiveness of public education in promoting tolerance for diversity.

TRENDS IN RACIAL AND ETHNIC RELATIONS

The new national mood of conservatism comes at a time of change and uncertainty in intergroup relations. In contrast with the recent past, when riots were nearly an annual occurrence in some inner cities and a "white backlash" produced forty-six electoral votes for an avowedly racist third-party presidential candidate, race relations in the early 1980s had receded somewhat as an issue of general concern. Nevertheless, there were numerous signs that the current calm might be short-lived. For one thing, extremist groups, such as the Ku Klux Klan and the American Nazi party, were taking a much more active and visible role in expressing hostility toward blacks, Jews, and other minorities. Perhaps not coincidentally, there was an increasing frequency of physical attacks on minority persons and property, including cross burnings at a number of northeastern colleges, defacement of synagogues in the New York area, a series of assaults on blacks in several southern states, and apparently random shootings of blacks in Salt Lake, New York, and other cities. Another barrier to the stabilization of intergroup relations was the continuing social and economic marginality of blacks and other racial minorities. For example, the median income of blacks in 1979 was only 56 percent of that of whites,[17] and rising rates of inflation and unemployment threatened to put blacks at a further disadvantage. Greatly complicating the prospects for social equality has been the annual influx of hundreds of thousands of legal immigrants, and at least as many illegal immigrants, into the United States. As discussed in chapter 6, the overwhelming majority of these newcomers are from Third World nations that had been effectively excluded under previous immigration policies. Thus, the new arrivals are not easily absorbed into existing communities and tend to remain relatively insulated from the mainstream of society. In addition, these Asian and Latin American immigrants are often lacking in education and job skills and have added to the strain on social services in some areas.

The prospect for intergroup relations in the years ahead, therefore, is not promising. One sociological rule of thumb is that intolerance is partly a product of hard times. Given the current state of the American economy, particularly the erosion of the industrial base in the Northeast and Midwest, a decline in relations between blacks and whites would not be unexpected. However, the most explosive conditions may well exist among minority groups, as native blacks and Hispanics are forced into competition with each other and with the burgeoning immigrant population for increasingly scarce social services, housing, and jobs.

The necessity of processing large numbers of poor, unskilled immigrants and of dealing with the economic dislocation and intergroup tension that sometimes result is by no means a new experience for the United States. Nor did all of the previous waves of immigration conveniently arrive at peak periods of economic prosperity. The assumption, then, is that American society will as before, "muddle through." One bothersome thought, however, is that Americans have come to rely heavily on public agencies, including the schools, to smooth out conflicts between groups. Thus, the present period of contraction in government seems especially ill-timed and likely to increase the problem of restoring the social equilibrium.

CONCLUSION

What has been offered in this chapter is a mixed bag of forecasts for the immediate future of tolerance socialization in the schools. On the one hand, some of the current actions of the federal government are possibly less threatening than might initially seem to be the case. Quite conceivably, certain social programs can be curtailed with little damage to citizenship training. The consequences of other proposed policy shifts, however, could prove to be devastating. Overall, the convergence of several trends, including budgetary reductions, federal "deregulation" of education, the movement toward desecularized schools, and the likelihood of increased racial and ethnic tension, offers the disturbing prospect that public education will be forced to do less to promote tolerance for diversity at a time when more efforts will be needed.

Under these circumstances, public schools will require the assistance of other agencies of socialization. In recent years, Americans have become both more and less dependent on schools for preparing each new generation for its place in society. We are told that families are now less directly involved in the socialization process, as parents, grandparents, and other adult relatives have fewer opportunities to be with children, and that the school has come to fill some of the vacuum.[18] Thus, elementary and secondary schools now offer instruction in areas that were once the province of the family, including sex education, values clarification, recreation, driver education, and so forth. At the same time, parents are also turning to other institutions for help. The most important case in point seems to be day care. With the steadily rising divorce rate and the burgeoning labor-force participation of married women, the enrollment of children in preschools, all-day centers, and other custodial agencies has increased dramatically. Accordingly, these agencies may supplement the elementary school's efforts to introduce the child to the ways of the larger society. In some circumstances, this could include rudimentary lessons in functional tolerance. However, the latter prospect is dimmed by the relatively exclusive admissions policies of some private day-care centers. Tuition charges may exclude some lower-income families, while the tendency of many agencies to draw enrollments primarily from a single neighborhood or from the membership lists of a sponsoring church may further reduce social diversity.

All of this should serve to remind us that the ultimate responsibility for promoting tolerance for diversity lies not with day-care centers, or with the schools, but with American society itself. Agencies of socialization are expected to transmit or reproduce the existing culture, not create a new one. Instead, the most effective approach to the socialization of tolerance would be for governments to insist that standards of fairness and equality are carried out in all major institutions. A good place to start would be the housing market. Although some progress has been made in recent years with the movement of substantial numbers of blacks and other minorities into suburbs that were once closed to them, residential segregation continues to be pervasive.[19] Thus, as things stand now, most children, and for that matter, most adults, experience social diversity in only one part of their lives. The larger question, of course, is whether Americans are truly interested in making society more tolerant, and if so, whether they are willing to make the changes and sacrifices that tolerance sometimes requires. History would suggest that our collective tolerance has its limits. Current experience indicates that, for the moment at least, those limits are not going to be appreciably extended.

Notes
Bibliography
Index

Notes

Chapter 1: Diversity and Its Consequences

1. Alexis de Tocqueville, *Democracy in America*, vol. I (New York: Colonial, 1899), p. 191.
2. U.S., Bureau of Census, *Statistical Abstract of the United States: 1979*, 100th ed. (Washington, D.C., 1979), table 79.
3. *World Almanac and Book of Facts, 1976* (New York: Newspaper Enterprise Association, 1976), pp. 373–386.
4. William Newman, *American Pluralism* (New York: Harper & Row, 1973).
5. Pierre van den Berghe, *Race and Racism: A Comparative Perspective*, 2nd ed. (New York: Wiley, 1978), Introduction.
6. Ibid.
7. Ibid., pp. xix–xx.
8. Milton Gordon, "Toward a General Theory of Racial and Ethnic Group Relations," in *Ethnicity*, ed. N. Glazer and D. P. Moynihan (Cambridge, Mass.: Harvard University Press, 1975).
9. Ibid., p. 107.
10. Glazer and Moynihan, *Ethnicity*, Introduction.
11. Harold Isaacs, "Basic Group Identity: The Idols of the Tribe," in *Ethnicity*, p. 54.
12. Useful sources for the contending points of view on this issue include Robert Dahl, *Pluralist Democracy in the United States: Conflict and Consensus* (Chicago: Rand McNally, 1967); Thomas Dye and L. Harmon Zeigler, *The Irony of Democracy*, 2nd ed. (Belmont, Calif.: Duxbury, 1972); and P. Bachrach, *The Theory of Democratic Elitism: A Critique* (Boston: Little, Brown, 1968).
13. Glazer and Moynihan, *Ethnicity*.
14. Daniel Selakovitch, *Ethnicity and the Schools* (Danville, Ill.: Interstate, 1978), p. 134.
15. Melvin Tumin, Introduction to *Pluralism in a Democratic Society*, ed. M. Tumin and W. Plotch (New York: Praeger, 1977), p. xii.
16. Discussions of the various models of intergroup relations can be found in a number of sources, including Charles Tesconi, *School-*

ing in America (Boston: Houghton Mifflin, 1975), chap. 11; and Mark Krug, *The Melting of the Ethnics* (Bloomington, Ind.: Phi Delta Kappa, 1976).

17. van den Berghe, *Race and Racism*.
18. See, for example, James Banks, "The Implications of Multicultural Education for Teacher Education," in *Pluralism and the American Teacher*, ed. F. Klassen and D. Gollnick (Washington, D.C.: Association of Colleges for Teacher Education, Ethnic Heritage Center, 1977).
19. Robert P. Wolff, "Beyond Tolerance," in *A Critique of Pure Tolerance*, ed. R. P. Wolff, B. Moore, and H. Marcuse (Boston: Beacon, 1975).
20. Irving Brant, *The Bill of Rights: Its Origin and Meaning* (New York: Mentor, 1965).
21. Brown v. Board of Education, 347 U.S. 483 (1954); Plessy v. Ferguson, 163 U.S. 537 (1896).
22. "The World Is Just Around the Corner in the Charlotte-Mecklenburg Schools" (pamphlet). Charlotte, N.C.: Charlotte-Mecklenburg Schools.

Chapter 2: Socialization for Diversity: The Conventional Wisdom

1. John Dewey, *Democracy and Education* (New York: Free Press, 1966), p. 23.
2. Thomas Jefferson, "The General Diffusion of Knowledge," in *Crusade Against Ignorance: Thomas Jefferson on Education*, ed. G. C. Lee (New York: Teachers College Press, 1961), p. 84.
3. See, for example, Paul Violas, *The Training of the Urban Working Class* (Chicago: Rand McNally, 1978).
4. Lawrence Cremin, *The Republic and the School: Horace Mann on the Education of Free Men* (New York: Teachers College Press, 1957), p. 80.
5. Henry Steele Commager, "Our Schools Have Kept Us Free," *Life*. October 16, 1950.
6. Brown v. Board of Education, 347 U.S. 483 (1954) at 493.
7. Lewis Coser, "Emile Durkheim," in *Masters of Sociological Thought*, 2nd ed. (New York: Harcourt, 1977), p. 132. See also Durkheim's major writings on this topic, *Education and Sociology* (Glencoe, Ill.:

Free Press, 1956) and *Moral Education* (New York: Free Press, 1962).

8. James Coleman et al., *Youth: Transition to Adulthood*, Report of the Panel on Youth of the President's Science Advisory Committee (Chicago: University of Chicago Press, 1974).

9. Sloan Wayland, "Interrelationship Between School Districts," in *The School in Society*, ed. S. Sieber and D. Wilder (New York: Free Press, 1973), p. 230.

10. For varying perspectives on the schools' contributions to the integration of the immigrants, see Colin Greer, *The Great School Legend* (New York: Viking, 1972); and Diane Ravitch, *The Revisionists Revised* (New York: Basic, 1978), especially chap. 5.

11. Some of this literature is discussed in George Simpson and J. Milton Yinger, *Racial and Cultural Minorities*, 4th ed. (New York: Harper & Row, 1972).

12. T. W. Adorno et al., *The Authoritarian Personality* (New York: Harper & Row, 1950), p. 971.

13. This interpretation is summarized in Mark Chesler, "Contemporary Sociological Theories of Racism," in *Toward the Elimination of Racism*, ed. P. Katz (New York: Pergamon, 1976).

14. Seymour Lipset and Earl Raab, *The Politics of Unreason* (New York: Harper & Row, 1970), p. 431.

15. Pierre van den Berghe, *Race and Racism: A Comparative Perspective*, 2nd ed. (New York: Wiley, 1978), chap. 4.

16. S. Gaertner, "Nonreactive Measures in Racial Attitude Research: A Focus on Liberals," in *Toward the Elimination of Racism*.

17. van den Berghe, *Race and Racism*, chap. 4.

18. U.S., Bureau of the Census, *Statistical Abstract of the United States*, 1981, 102nd ed. (Washington, D.C., 1981), table 232.

19. Adorno et al., *The Authoritarian Personality*; Gunnar Myrdahl, *An American Dilemma* (New York: Harper & Row, 1954); Robin M. Williams, *The Reduction of Intergroup Tensions* (New York: Social Science Research Council, 1947); Gordon Allport, *The Nature of Prejudice* (Reading, Mass.: Addison-Wesley, 1954).

20. Samuel Stouffer, *Communism, Conformity, and Civil Liberties* (New York: Doubleday, 1955).

21. James Prothro and Charles Grigg, "Fundamental Principles of Democracy: Bases of Agreement and Disagreement," *Journal of Politics* 22 (1960): 276–294; Herbert McCloskey, "Consensus and Ideology in American Politics," *American Political Science Review*

58 (1964): 361–382; Lipset and Raab, *Politics of Unreason*; Darrel Montero, "Support for Civil Liberties Among a Cohort of High School Graduates and College Students," *Journal of Social Issues* 31, no. 2 (1975): 123–136; James Davis, "Communism, Conformity, Cohorts and Categories: American Tolerance in 1954 and 1972–73," *American Journal of Sociology* 81 (1975): 491–513; Clyde Nunn, Harry Crockett, and J. Allen Williams, *Tolerance for Non-conformity* (San Francisco: Jossey-Bass, 1978); Herbert Hyman and Charles Wright, *Education's Lasting Influence on Values* (Chicago: University of Chicago Press, 1979).

22. R. M. Williams, *Strangers Next Door* (Englewood Cliffs, N.J.: Prentice-Hall, 1964); Bruno Bettelheim and Morris Janowitz, *Social Change and Prejudice* (New York: Free Press, 1964); Gertrude Selznick and Stephen Steinberg, *The Tenacity of Prejudice* (New York: Harper & Row, 1969); Lipset and Raab, *Politics of Unreason*; Hyman and Wright, *Education's Lasting Influence on Values*.

23. The strongest evidence on this point is presented in the studies of Hyman and Wright, Davis, and Nunn and associates, all of which are cited in note 21, above.

24. *Cardinal Principles of Secondary Education: Bureau of Education Bulletin No. 35* (Washington, D.C.: Department of the Interior, 1918); reprinted in *The Development of Secondary Education*, ed. F. Raubinger et al. (London: Macmillan, 1969).

25. George Gallup, "The Eleventh Annual Gallup Poll of the Public's Attitudes Toward the Public Schools," *Phi Delta Kappan* 61 (1979): 33–45.

26. Edgar Litt, "Civic Education, Community Norms, and Political Indoctrination," *American Sociological Review* 28 (1963): 69–75.

27. Kenneth Langton and M. Kent Jennings, "Political Socialization and the High School Civics Curriculum in the United States," *American Political Science Review* 62 (1968): 852–867.

28. M. Kent Jennings, Kenneth Langton, and Richard Niemi, "Effects of High School Civics Curriculum," in *The Political Character of Adolescence*, ed. M. K. Jennings and R. Niemi (Princeton, N.J.: Princeton University Press, 1974).

29. Byron Massialas, *Education and the Political System* (Reading, Mass.: Addison-Wesley, 1969); Dennis Goldenson, "An Alternative View About the Role of the Secondary School in Political Socialization," *Theory and Research in Social Education* 6 (1978): 44–72.

30. Gail Zellman and David Sears, "Childhood Origins of Tolerance for Dissent," *Journal of Social Issues* 27, no. 1 (1971): 109–136; Goldenson, "An Alternative View."

31. Lee Ehman, "An Analysis of the Relationships of Selected Educational Variables with the Political Socialization of High School Students," *American Education Research Journal* 6 (1969): 559–580.

32. Goldenson, "An Alternative View."

33. Lee Ehman, "The American School in the Political Socialization Process," *Review of Educational Research* 50 (1980): 99–119.

34. Judith V. Torney, A. N. Oppenheim, and Russell F. Farnen, *Civic Education in Ten Countries* (New York: Wiley, 1975); H. D. Neilsen, *Tolerating Political Dissent* (Stockholm: Almqvist & Wiksell, 1977).

35. M. Kent Jennings, Lee Ehman, and Richard Niemi, "Social Studies Teachers and Their Pupils," in *The Political Character of Adolescence*, p. 224.

36. Richard Dawson and Kenneth Prewitt, *Political Socialization* (Boston: Little, Brown, 1969).

37. Joseph Adelson and Robert O'Neill, "Growth of Political Ideas in Adolescence: The Sense of Community," *Journal of Personality and Social Psychology* 4 (1966): 295–306; Richard Merelman, *Political Socialization and Educational Climates* (New York: Holt, Rinehart & Winston, 1971); Judith V. Torney, "Socialization of Attitudes Toward the Legal System," *Journal of Social Issues* 27 (1971): 137–154.

38. Merelman, *Political Socialization*; Torney, Oppenheim, and Farnen, *Civic Education*; Robert C. Serow and Kenneth Strike, "Students' Attitudes Towards High School Governance: Implications for Social Education," *Theory and Research in Social Education* 6, no. 3 (1978): 12–26; Neilsen, *Tolerating Political Dissent*.

39. Neilsen, *Tolerating Political Dissent*.

40. James Coleman, *The Adolescent Society* (New York: Free Press, 1961); C. W. Gordon, *The Social System of the High School* (Glencoe, Ill.: Free Press, 1957); A. B. Hollingshead, *Elmstown's Youth* (New York: Wiley, 1949); Willard Waller, *The Sociology of Teaching* (New York: Wiley, 1967).

41. Neilsen, *Tolerating Political Dissent*; Torney, Oppenheim, and Farnen, *Civic Education*.

42. Kenneth Langton, *Political Socialization* (New York: Oxford University Press, 1969).

43. Martin Levin, "Social Climates and Political Socialization," in

Learning About Politics, ed. R. Sigel (New York: Random House, 1970).

44. Robert Frederick, *The Third Curriculum* (New York: Appleton, 1959); Joseph Roemer and Charles Allen, *Extra-curricular Activities in Junior and Senior High Schools* (New York: Heath, 1926).
45. Merelman, *Political Socialization*; Serow and Strike, "Students' Attitudes."
46. Samuel Bowles and Herbert Gintis, *Schooling in Capitalist America* (New York: Basic, 1976); E. Morgan, *Inequality in Classroom Learning* (New York: Praeger, 1977).
47. Madelaine Rafalides and Wayne Hoy, "Student Sense of Alienation and Pupil Control Orientation of High Schools," *High School Journal* 55 (1971): 101–111.
48. Morgan, *Inequality in Classroom Learning*.
49. Theophilus Odetola et al., "Organizational Structure and Student Alienation," *Educational Administration Quarterly* 8 (1972): 15–26; Barry Anderson, "School Bureaucratization and Alienation from the High School," *Sociology of Education* 46 (1973): 315–334.
50. Edward Suchman, John Dean, and Robin M. Williams, *Desegregation: Some Propositions and Research Suggestions* (New York: Antidefamation League of B'nai Brith, 1958).
51. Elizabeth Cohen, "The Effects of Desegregation on Race Relations," *Law and Contemporary Problems* 39 (1975): 272.
52. Phyllis Katz, "Attitude Change in Children: Can the Twig Be Straightened?" in *Toward the Elimination of Racism*.
53. Ibid.; Harold Proshansky, "The Development of Intergroup Attitudes," in *Review of Child Development Research*, ed. L. W. Hoffman and M. L. Hoffman (New York: Russell Sage Foundation, 1966).
54. Allport, *Nature of Prejudice*; R. M. Williams, *Reduction of Intergroup Tensions*.
55. Martha Carithers, "School Desegregation and Racial Cleavage, 1954–1970: A Review of the Literature," *Journal of Social Issues* 26, no. 4 (1970): 25–47; Cohen, "Effects of Desegregation"; N. St. John, *School Desegregation: Outcomes for Children* (New York: Wiley, 1975); Yehuda Amir,"The Role of Intergroup Contact in Change of Prejudice and Ethnic Relations," in *Towards the Elimination of Racism*; Janet Schofield, "School Desegregation and Intergroup Relations," in *Social Psychology of Education*, ed D. Bar-Tal and L. Saxe (Washington, D.C.: Hemisphere, 1978).

56. St. John, *School Desegregation*.

57. Christine Bennett, "Interracial Acceptance in Desegregated Schools," *Phi Delta Kappan* 60 (1979): 683–684; Harold Gerard and Norman Miller, *School Desegregation* (New York: Plenum, 1975); Nancy St. John and Ralph Lewis, "Children's Interracial Friendships: An Exploration of the Contact Hypothesis" (unpublished, cited in N. St. John, *School Desegregation: Outcomes for Children* [New York: Wiley, 1975]); David DeVries and Keith Edwards, "Student Teams and Learning Games: Their Effects on Cross-race and Cross-sex Interaction," *Journal of Education Psychology* 66 (1974): 741–749; Russell Weigel, Patricia Wiser and Stuart Cook, "The Impact of Cooperative Learning Experiences on Cross-ethnic Relations and Attitudes," *Journal of Social Issues* 31 (1975): 229–244; Elliot Aronson, Diane Bridgeman and Robert Gefner, "The Effects of a Cooperative Classroom Structure on Student Behavior and Attitudes," in *Social Psychology of Education*; Robert C. Serow and Daniel Solomon, "Classroom Climates and Students' Intergroup Behavior," *Journal of Educational Psychology* 71 (1979): 669–676.

58. The clearest illustration of the effects of teacher presence on students' intergroup behaviors can be found in Ray C. Rist, ed., *Desegregated Schools: Appraisals of an American Experiment* (New York: Academic, 1979). Of particular interest are the following reports: Dorothy Clement, Margaret Eisenhart, and Joe C. Harding, "Social-Race Relations in a Southern Desegregated School"; Thomas Collins, "From Courtrooms to Classrooms: Managing School Desegregation in a Deep South High School"; and Janet Schofield, and H. Andrew Sagar, "The Social Context of Learning in an Interracial School."

59. Thomas Dye and L. Harmon Zeigler, *The Irony of Democracy*, 2nd ed. (Belmont, Calif.: Duxbury, 1972), p. 41.

60. Montero, "Support for Civil Liberties."

61. Kenneth Feldman and Theodore Newcomb, *The Impact of College on Students* (San Francisco: Jossey-Bass, 1969).

62. Montero, "Support for Civil Liberties"; Nunn, Crockett, and Williams, *Tolerance for Non-conformity*; Stouffer, *Communism, Conformity, and Civil Liberties*; Williams, *Strangers Next Door*.

63. Hyman and Wright, *Education's Lasting Influence on Values*.

64. This point is effectively made in several of the studies of high school peer groups cited in 40, especially those of Waller and

Gordon. For the possible long-range goals of the extra curriculum, see the discussion in Violas, *Training of the Urban Working Class*, chap. 5.

Chapter 3: Education and Tolerance: A Reappraisal

1. Thomas Kuhn, *The Structure of Scientific Revolutions* (Chicago: University of Chicago Press, 1963).
2. Clyde Nunn, Harry Crockett, and J. Allen Williams, *Tolerance for Non-conformity* (San Francisco: Jossey-Bass, 1978), chap 4. For a similar argument, see M. Trow, "Small Businessmen, Political Tolerance, and Support for McCarthy," *American Journal of Sociology* 54 (1958): 270–281.
3. Jane Ferrar, "The Dimensions of Tolerance," *Pacific Sociological Review* 19 (1976): 63–81.
4. Lewis Coser, *Masters of Sociological Thought*, 2nd ed. (New York: Harcourt Brace Jovanovich, 1977); J. Karabel and A. H. Halsey, "Educational Research: A Review and an Interpretation," in *Power and Ideology in Education*, ed. J. Karabel and A. H. Halsey (New York: Oxford University Press, 1977).
5. Richard LaPiere, "Attitudes v. Actions," *Social Forces* 13 (1934): 237.
6. Nancy St. John, *School Desegregation: Outcomes for Children* (New York: Wiley, 1975).
7. Robert Merton, "Fact and Factitiousness in Ethnic Opinionnaires," *American Sociological Review* 5 (1940): 13–28.
8. Irwin Deutscher, "Words and Deeds: Social Science and Social Policy," *Social Problems* 13 (1966): 235–254.
9. Milton Rokeach, "Attitudes: The Nature of Attitudes," in *International Encyclopedia of the Social Sciences*, vol. 16 (New York: Macmillan and Free Press, 1968).
10. Deutscher, "Words and Deeds."
11. Allan Wicker, "Attitudes v. Actions: The Relationship of Verbal and Overt Behavioral Responses to Attitude Objects," *Journal of Social Issues* 25, no. 4 (1969): 41–78.
12. A comprehensive analysis of the entire attitude-behavior issue, including the technical problems, can be found in Irwin Deutscher, *What We Say/What We Do* (Glenview, Ill.: Scott, Foresman, 1973).

13. La Piere, "Attitudes v. Actions"; Wicker, "Attitudes v. Actions"; H. McCloskey, "Consensus and Ideology in American Politics," *American Political Science Review* 58 (1964): 361–382; J. Prothro and C. Grigg, "Fundamental Principles of Democracy: Bases of Agreement and Disagreement," *Journal of Politics* 22 (1960): 276–294.

14. Phyllis Katz, "Attitude Change in Children: Can the Twig Be Straightened?" in *Toward the Elimination of Racism*, ed. P. A. Katz (New York: Pergamon, 1976).

15. Katz, "Attitude Change in Children"; G. Simpson, and J. Milton Yinger, *Racial and Cultural Minorities*, 4th ed. (New York: Harper & Row, 1972).

16. Stanley Renshon, "Assumptive Frameworks in Political Socialization Theory," in *Handbook of Political Socialization: Theory and Research*, ed. S. Renshon (New York: Free Press, 1977).

17. Joseph Adelson and Robert O'Neill, "Growth of Political Ideas in Adolescence: The Sense of Community," *Journal of Personality and Social Psychology* 4 (1966): 295–306; Richard Merelman, *Political Socialization and Educational Climates* (New York: Holt, Rinehart & Winston, 1971); June Tapp and Lawrence Kohlberg, "Developing Senses of Law and Legal Justice," *Journal of Social Issues* 27 (1971): 65–92; J. Torney, "Socialization of Attitudes Toward the Legal System," *Journal of Social Issues* 27 (1971): 137–154.

18. Florence Davidson, "Respect for Persons and Ethnic Prejudice in Childhood: A Cognitive-developmental Prescription," in *Pluralism in a Democratic Society*, ed. M. Tumin and W. Plotch (New York: Praeger, 1977).

19. Alexis de Tocqueville, *Democracy in America*, vol. 2 (New York: Knopf, 1956), p. 8.

20. David Easton, *A Systems Analysis of Political Life* (New York: Wiley, 1965); David Easton and Robert Hess, "The Child's Political World," *Midwest Journal of Political Science* 6 (1962): 229–246.

21. Talcott Parsons, *The Social System* (Glencoe, Ill.: Free Press, 1951).

22. McCloskey, "Consensus and Ideology."

23. Prothro and Grigg, "Fundamental Principles of Democracy"; Gail Zellman, "Antidemocratic Beliefs: A Survey and Some Explanations," *Journal of Social Issues* 31 (1975): 31–54.

24. Robin M. Williams, *Mutual Accommodation* (Minneapolis: Univer-

sity of Minnesota Press, 1977); "Whites Grow Reluctant to Back Integration Steps," *New York Times*, 2 December 1979.

25. Thomas Dye and L. Harmon Zeigler, *The Irony of Democracy*, 2nd ed. (Belmont, Calif.: Duxbury, 1972), p. 184.

26. Prothro and Grigg, "Fundamental Principles of Democracy"; McCloskey, "Consensus and Ideology"; Nunn, Crockett, and Williams, "Tolerance for Non-conformity;" S. Stouffer, *Communism, Conformity and Civil Liberties* (New York: Doubleday, 1955).

27. Robert Dahl, *Pluralist Democracy in the United States: Conflict and Consensus* (Chicago: Rand McNally, 1967).

28. Dye and Zeigler, *Irony of Democracy*.

29. Peter Bachrach, *The Theory of Democratic Elitism: A Critique* (Boston: Little, Brown, 1968), p. 36.

30. Seymour Lipset and Earl Raab, *The Politics of Unreason* (New York: Harper & Row, 1970), p. 431.

31. Pierre van den Berghe, *Race and Racism: A Comparative Perspective*, 2nd ed. (New York: Wiley, 1978), p. 138.

32. Orlando Patterson, "On Guilt, Relativism, and Black-White Relations," *American Scholar* 43 (1973): 122.

33. Williams, *Mutual Accomodation;* U.S., Commission on Civil Rights, *Fulfilling the Letter and the Spirit of the Law* (Washington, D.C.: U.S., Commission on Civil Rights, 1976).

34. Richard Pratte, "Cultural Diversity and Education," in *Ethics and Educational Policy*, ed. K. Strike and K. Egan (London: Routledge & Kegan Paul, 1978).

35. Elizabeth Cohen, "The Effects of Desegregation on Race Relations," *Law and Contemporary Problems* 39 (1975): 273.

36. Robert C. Serow and Daniel Solomon, "Classroom Climates and Students' Intergroup Behavior," *Journal of Educational Psychology* 71 (1979): 669–676; C. Bennett, "International Acceptance in Desegregated Schools," *Phi Delta Kappan* 60 (1979): 683–684; David DeVries and Keith Edwards, "Student Teams and Learning Games: Their Effects on Cross-race and Cross-sex Interaction," *Journal of Educational Psychology* 66 (1974): 741–749; Russell Wiegel, Patricia Wiser, and Stuart Cook, "The Impact of Cooperative Learning Experiences on Cross-ethnic Relations and Attitudes," *Journal of Social Issues* 31 (1975) 219–244; Elliot Aronson, Diane Bridgeman, and Robert Gefner, "The Effects of a Cooperative Classroom Structure on Student Behavior and At-

titudes," in *Social Psychology of Education*, ed. D. Bar-Tal and L. Saxe (Washington, D.C.: Hemisphere, 1978).

37. Serow and Solomon, "Classroom Climates."
38. Steven Bossert, *Tasks and Social Relationships in Classrooms* (Cambridge: Cambridge University Press, 1979).
39. Emile Durkheim, *Education and Sociology* (Glencoe, Ill.: Free Press, 1956); idem, *Moral Education* (New York: Free Press, 1961).
40. Durkheim, *Moral Education*, pp. 147–153.
41. Ibid., p. 153.
42. Talcott Parsons, "The School Class as a Social System," *Harvard Educational Review* 29 (1959): 297–318.
43. Robert Dreeben, *On What Is Learned in School* (Reading, Mass.: Addison-Wesley, 1968).
44. Ibid., pp. 66–76.
45. Nathan Glazer, "Cultural Pluralism: The Social Aspect," in *Pluralism in a Democratic Society*, ed. M. Tumin and W. Plotch (New York: Praeger, 1977).
46. Phillip Jackson, *Life in Classrooms* (New York: Holt, Rinehart & Winston, 1968).
47. Dorothy Clement, Margaret Eisenhart, and Joe C. Harding, "The Veneer of Harmony: Social-race Relations in a Southern Desegregated School," in *Desegregated Schools*, ed. R. Rist (New York: Academic, 1979).
48. Ray C. Rist, "Student Social Class and Teacher Expectations: The Self-fulfilling Prophecy in Ghetto Education," *Harvard Educational Review* 40 (1970): 411–451.
49. Bossert, *Tasks and Social Relationships*.
50. Harold Gerard and Norman Miller, *School Desegregation* (New York: Plenum, 1975); Nancy St. John and Ralph Lewis, "Children's Interracial Friendships: An Exploration of the Contact Hypothesis" (unpublished; cited in St. John, *School Desegregation*).
51. Serow and Solomon, "Classroom Climates."
52. Clement, Eisenhart, and Harding, "Veneer of Harmony"; Janet Schofeld and H. Andrew Sagar, "The Social Context of Learning in an Interracial School," in *Desegregated Schools*.
53. Clement, Eisenhart, and Harding, "Veneer of Harmony," p. 60.
54. T. W. Adorno et al., *The Authoritarian Personality* (New York: Harper & Row, 1950).

55. Durkheim, *Moral Education*, p. 147.
56. Ibid., p. 149.
57. Parsons, "The Social System," pp. 207–226.
58. Ibid.; Harry Gracey, "Learning the Student Role: Kindergarten as Academic Boot Camp," in *The Sociology of Education: A Source Book*, 3rd ed., ed. H. Stub (Homewood, Ill.: Dorsey, 1975).
59. Parsons, "The School Class," pp 305–307.
60. M. Kent Jennings and Richard Niemi, *The Political Character of Adolescence* (Princeton, N.J.: Princeton University Press, 1974), chap. 3.
61. Richard Dawson and Kenneth Prewitt, *Political Socialization* (Boston: Little, Brown, 1969), pp. 168–169.
62. Martin Patchen et al., "Determinants of Students' Interracial Behavior and Opinion Change," *Sociology of Education* 50 (1977): 55–75; U.S., Commission on Civil Rights, *Racial Isolation in the Public Schools* (Washington, D.C.: U.S., Commission on Civil Rights, 1967).
63. Jomills Braddock, "The Perpetuation of Segregation across Levels of Education: A Behavioral Assessment of the Contact Hypothesis," *Sociology of Education* 53 (1980): 178–186.
64. Nathan Glazer, *Affirmative Discrimination* (New York: Basic, 1978), p. 200.
65. Robin M. Williams, *Mutual Accomodation*.

Chapter 4: An Analytic Framework for Students' Intergroup Relations

1. U.S., Commission on Civil Rights, *Fulfilling the Letter and Spirit of the Law: Desegregation of the Nation's Public Schools* (U.S., Commission on Civil Rights 1976), p. 293.
2. Lawrence Kohlberg, "Stage and Sequence: The Cognitive-developmental Approach to Socialization," in *Handbook of Socialization Theory and Research*, ed. D. Goslin (Chicago: Rand McNally, 1969).
3. Ibid., p. 369.
4. Ibid., p. 390.
5. Ibid., pp. 376ff.
6. Ibid.
7. Kohlberg, as quoted in John Patrick, "Political Socialization and Political Education in Schools" in *Handbook of Political Socializa-*

tion: Theory and Research, ed. S. Renshon (New York: Free Press, 1977), p. 210.

8. June Tapp and Lawrence Kohlberg, "Developing Senses of Law and Legal Justice," *Journal of Social Issues* 27, no. 2 (1971): 65–92.

9. Florence Davidson, "Respect for Persons and Ethnic Prejudice in Childhood: A Cognitive-developmental Description," in *Pluralism in a Democratic Society*, ed. M. Tumin and W. Plotch (New York: Praeger, 1977).

10. Evidence concerning applications of the Kohlberg model may be found in John Gibbs, "Kohlberg's Stages of Moral Judgment: A Constructive Critique," in *Stage Theories of Cognitive and Moral Development: Criticisms and Applications*, Harvard Educational Review Reprint no. 13, 1978.

11. Samuel Gaertner, "Nonreactive Measures in Racial Attitude Research: A Focus on Liberals," in *Towards the Elimination of Racism*, ed. P. Katz (New York: Pergamon, 1976).

12. Nancy St. John, *School Desegregation: Outcomes for Children* (New York: Wiley, 1975).

13. Gary Orfield, "How to Make Desegregation Work: The Adaptation of Schools to Their Newly-integrated Student Bodies," *Law and Contemporary Problems* 39 (1975): 314–340.

14. Dorothy Clement, Margaret Eisenhart, and Joe C. Harding, "The Veneer of Harmony: Social-race Relations in a Southern Desegregated School," in *Desegregated Schools: Appraisals of an American Experiment*, ed. R. Rist (New York: Academic, 1979).

15. Janet Schofield and H. Andrew Sagar, "The Social Context of Learning in an Interracial School," in *Desegregated Schools*.

16. Kohlberg, "Stage and Sequence"; Gibbs, "Kohlberg's Stages of Moral Judgement"; Clement, Eisenhart, and Harding, "Veneer of Harmony"; Schofield and Sagar, "Social Context of Learning"; Thomas Collins, "From Courtrooms to Classrooms: Managing School Desegregation in a Deep South High School," in *Desegregated Schools*.

17. Howard Husock, "Boston: The Problem That Won't Go Away," *New York Times Magazine*, 25 November 1979.

18. Clement, Eisenhart, and Harding, "Veneer of Harmony"; Schofield and Sagar, "Social Context of Learning"; Collins, "From Courtrooms to Classrooms."

19. Collins, "From Courtrooms to Classrooms."

20. Schofield and Sagar, "Social Context of Learning."

21. For a review of these findings, see chapters 2 and 3.

22.. Schofield and Sagar, "Social Context of Learning."

23. For a discussion of norms and values, see Robin M. Williams, "Values: The Concept of Values"; and Milton Rokeach, "Attitudes: The Nature of Attitudes," in *International Encyclopedia of the Social Sciences*, vol. 16 (New York: Macmillan and Free Press, 1968).

24. U.S., Commission on Civil Rights, *Fulfilling the Letter*.

25. See, for instance, Orfield, "How to Make Desegregation Work."

26. Schofield and Sagar, "Social Context of Learning."

27. Williams, "Values"; Rokeach, "Attitudes."

28. Montgomery County (Md.) Public Schools, *Evaluation of the 1976–77 Desegregation Program in the Montgomery County Public Schools* (Rockville, Md., 1978).

29. Kohlberg, "Stage and Sequence"; Tapp and Kohlberg, "Developing Senses of Law."

30. Johannes Pennings, "Measures of Organizational Structure: A Methodological Note," *American Journal of Sociology* 79 (1973): 686–704. See also James Lincoln and Gerald Zeitz, "Organizational Properties from Aggregate Data: Separating Individual from Structural Effects," *American Sociological Review* 45 (1980): 391–408.

31. Williams, "Values," p. 285.

32. Clement, Eisenhart, and Harding, "Veneer of Harmony"; Schofield and Sagar, "Social Context of Learning."

33. Paul Breer and Edwin Locke, *Task Experience as a Source of Attitudes* (Homewood, Ill.: Dorsey, 1965).

34. Gabriel Almond and Stanley Verba, *The Civic Culture* (Boston: Little, Brown, 1965).

35. Eigel Pederson and Therese A. Faucher, with William Eaton, "A New Perspective on the Effects of First-grade Teachers on Children's Subsequent Adult Status," *Harvard Educational Review* 48 (1978): 1–31.

Chapter 5: Mainstreaming the Handicapped

1. An excellent summary and discussion of P.L. 94-142 can be found in Leroy Goodman's article "A Bill of Rights for the Handicapped" (*American Education*, November 1976; reprinted in *Readings in Special Education, 1978/79* [Guilford, Conn.: Special Learning Corp., 1978]).

2. The term *mainstreaming* has had a variety of uses and is currently the subject of some disagreement among special educators. Nevertheless, it is most commonly used to describe the integration of handicapped children within regular classes. See, for instance, James Paul, Ann Turnbull, and William Cruickshank, *Mainstreaming: A Practical Guide* (Syracuse, N.Y.: Syracuse University Press, 1977).

3. U.S., Department of Health, Education, and Welfare, *Progress Toward a Free Appropriate Public Education* (Washington, D.C.: GPO, 1979), table D-2.2, p. 169.

4. U.S., Bureau of the Census, *Statistical Abstract of the United States*,1979, 100th ed. (Washington, D.C.: U.S., Bureau of the Census, 1979), tables 243 and 244, p. 151.

5. Ibid., table 245, p. 152.

6. National Center for Educational Statistics, *The Condition of Education, 1976 edition* (Washington, D.C.: GPO, 1976), table 1.3, p. 178.

7. According to the 1980 census, 85.5 percent of young American adults (24-35 years of age) have completed high school. U.S., Bureau of the Census, *Statistical Abstract of the United States, 1981*, 102nd ed. (Washington, D.C.: U.S., Bureau of the Census, 1981), table 230, p. 141.

8. This discussion of the history of mainstreaming and racial desegregation draws heavily on the following: Maynard Reynolds and Sylvia Rosen, "Special Education: Past, Present, and Future," in *Readings in Special Education, 1978/79* (Guilford, Conn.: Special Learning Corp., 1978); Thomas Gilhool, "Changing Public Policies: Roots and Forces," *Minnesota Education* 2 (1976): 8–14; Meyer Weinberg, *A Chance to Learn* (Cambridge: Cambridge University Press, 1977); E. Zelder, "Public Opinion and Public Education for the Handicapped Child—Court Decisions 1873–1950," *Exceptional Children* 19 (1953): 187–198.

9. Plessy v. Ferguson, 163 U.S. 537 (1896).

10. Weinberg, *Chance to Learn*.

11. Bill Gearhart and Mel Weishahn, *The Handicapped Child in the Regular Classroom* (St. Louis: Mosby, 1976); Daniel Hallahan and James Kauffman, *Exceptional Children: Introduction to Special Education* (Englewood Cliffs, N.J.: Prentice-Hall, 1978).

12. Pennsylvania Association for Retarded Children v. Pennsylvania, 334 F. Supp. 1257 (1971).

13. Brown v. Board of Education, 347 U.S. 483 (1954).

14. The most influential statement of this type was Lloyd Dunn's article, "Special Education for the Mildly Retarded: Is Much of It Justifiable?" *Exceptional Children* 35 (1968): 5–22.
15. National Center for Educational Statistics, *Condition of Education, 1976*, table 3.16, p. 214.
16. The Court's position on this matter was originally set forth in Milliken v. Bradley, 418 U.S. 717 (1974).
17. Brown v. Board of Education.
18. Frank T. Read, "Judicial Evolution of the Law of School Integration since *Brown* v. *Board of Education*," *Law and Contemporary Problems* 39 (1975): 7–49.
19. L. Friedman, ed. *Argument: The Oral Argument Before the Supreme Court in Brown* v. *Board of Education of Topeka*, 1952–55 (New York: Chelsea House, 1969), p. 51., cited in Gilhool, "Changing Public Policies," p. 12.
20. Gilhool, "Changing Public Policies."
21. Diana v. State Board of Education, Civil Action No. C-70, 37 RFP (N.D. Cal. Jan. 7, 1970 and June 18, 1973).
22. Pennsylvania Association for Retarded Children v. Pensylvania.
23. Mills v. Board of Education of District of Columbia, 348 F. Supp. 866 (1972).
24. The "interracial transfer" argument appears widely in the desegregation literature. For a summary and critique, see Nancy St. John, *School Desegregation: Outcomes for Children* (New York: Wiley, 1975), chap. 5.
25. Clara Baldwin and Alfred Baldwin, "Personality and Social Development of Handicapped Children," in *Readings in Special Education, 1978/79.*
26. Gearhart and Weishahn, *Handicapped Child.*
27. David Goslin, *The School in Contemporary Society* (Glenview, Ill.: Scott, Foresman, 1965), chap. 4.
28. The concepts of reference groups and membership groups are discussed at length in Robert Merton, *Social Theory and Social Structure* (London: Free Press, 1964).
29. The interracial transfer-of-values thesis may be, by contemporary standards, somewhat patronizing toward blacks, insofar as it suggests that white students have a monopoly on desirable social values and behaviors. Keep in mind, however, that this argument was formulated during a period of intensive social reform (the 1960s), when the issues of race and social class were very often thought to be synonymous. Indeed, as St. John has pointed out,

the lateral transfer objective of desegregation actually pertains more to socioeconomic integration than to race (*School Desegregation*, chap. 5).

30. Thomas Pettigrew, "Racially Separate or Together," *Journal of Social Issues* 25, no. 1, (1969): 43–69.
31. Jay Gottlieb, Melvyn Semmel, and Donald Veldman, "Correlates of Social Status Among Mainstreamed Mentally Retarded Children," *Journal of Educational Psychology* 70 (1978): 396–405.
32. J. William Cook and Janet Wollersheim, "The Effect of Labeling of Special Education Students on the Perceptions of Contact Versus Noncontact Normal Peers," *Journal of Special Education* 10 (1976): 187–198.
33. Roger Johnson et al., "Interaction Between Handicapped and Nonhandicapped Teenagers as a Function of Situational Goal Structuring: Implications for Mainstreaming," *American Educational Research Journal* 16 (1979): 161–167.
34. Gottlieb, Semmel, and Veldman, "Correlates of Social Status."
35. Elizabeth Cohen, "The Effects of Desegregation on Race Relations," *Law and Contemporary Problems* 39 (1975): 271–299.
36. Gottlieb, Semmel, and Veldman, "Correlates of Social Status."
37. Francis Connor, Herbert Rusalem, and William Cruickshank, "Psychological Considerations of Crippled Children," in *Psychology of Exceptional Children and Youth*, ed. W. Cruickshank (Englewood Cliffs, N.J.: Prentice-Hall, 1971).
38. Gilhool, "Changing Public Policies"; Reynolds and Rosen, "Special Education."
39. David Milofsky, "Schooling the Kids No One Wants," *New York Times Magazine*, January 2, 1977.

Chapter 6: Multicultural Education

1. There have been numerous books and essays dealing with the current "ethnic revitalization." Of particular interest are the papers collected by Nathan Glazer and Daniel Patrick Moynihan in *Ethnicity* (Cambridge, Mass.: Harvard University Press, 1977).
2. Raymond Giles and Donna Gollnick, "Ethnic/cultural Diversity as Reflected in State and Federal Education Legislation and Policies," in *Pluralism and the American Teacher*, ed. F. Klassen and D. Gollnick (Washington, D.C.: American Association of Colleges for Teacher Education, Ethnic Heritage Center for Teacher Education, 1977), p. 127.

3. Ibid., p. 116.
4. Richard S. Schweiker, as quoted in S. La Guina and F. Cavaioli, *The Ethnic Dimension in American Society* (Boston: Holbrook, 1974), p. 4. These remarks are also cited in Giles and Gollnick, "Ethnic/Cultural Diversity," pp. 118–119.
5. Lau v. Nichols, 414 U.S. 563 (1974).
6. Giles and Gollnick, "Ethnic/cultural Diversity," p. 135.
7. American Association of Colleges for Teacher Education, "No One Model American," *Journal of Teacher Education* 24 (1974): 264–265.
8. Ibid.
9. Geneva Gay, "Curriculum for Multicultural Teacher Education," in *Pluralism and the American Teacher*.
10. Harold Proshansky, "The Development of Intergroup Attitudes," in *Review of Child Development Research*, ed. L. W. Hoffman and M. L. Hoffman (New York: Russell Sage Foundation, 1966); P. A. Katz, "Attitude Change in Children: Can the Twig be Straightened?" in *Toward the Elimination of Racism*, ed. P. A. Katz (New York: Pergamon, 1976).
11. Robin M. Williams, *The Reduction of Intergroup Tensions* (New York: Social Science Research Council, 1947); Gordon Allport, *The Nature of Prejudice* (Reading, Mass.: Addison-Wesley, 1954).
12. Dorothy Clement, Margaret Eisenhart, and Joe Harding, "The Veneer of Harmony: Social-race Relations in a Southern Desegregated School," and Janet Schofield and H. Andrew Sagar, "The Social Context of Learning in an Interracial School," both in *Desegregated Schools*, ed. R. Rist (New York: Academic, 1979).
13. Schofield and Sagar, "Social Context of Learning."
14. For one exposition of this argument, see Christine Bennett, "A Case for Pluralism in the Schools," *Phi Delta Kappan*, 62 (1981): 589–591.
15. Charles Tesconi, *Schooling in America* (Boston: Houghton Mifflin, 1975), p. 170.
16. Horace Kallen, *Culture and Democracy in the United States* (New York: Boni and Liveright, 1924), p. 43.
17. Pierre van den Berghe, *Race and Racism: A Comparative Perspective*, 2nd ed. (New York: Wiley, 1978), p. 147.
18. Thomas F. Green, "Education and Pluralism: Ideas and Reality," unpublished; quoted in Richard Pratte, "Cultural Diversity and

Education," in *Ethics and Educational Policy*, ed. K. Strike and K. Egan (London: Routledge & Kegan Paul, 1978).

19. See, for example, Christopher Lasch, *The Culture of Narcissism* (New York: Norton, 1979).

20. Pratte, "Cultural Diversity and Education"; N. Glazer and D. Moynihan, *Ethnicity* (Cambridge: Harvard University Press, 1977).

21. A useful source for statements of the multiculturalist position on this issue is *Cultural Pluralism in Education*, ed. M. Stent, W. Hazard, and H. Rivlin (New York: Appleton-Century-Crofts, 1973). See, in particular, the articles by Hazard and Stent and by Guerra.

22. Michael Novak, *The Rise of the Unmeltable Ethnics* (New York: Macmillan, 1971); John Ogbu, *Minority Education and Caste* (New York: Academic, 1977); Stent, Hazard and Rivlin, *Cultural Pluralism in Education*.

23. William Ryan, *Blaming the Victim* (New York: Random House, 1971), pp. 119–120.

24. Talcott Parsons, "Some Theoretical Considerations on the Nature and Trends of Change in Ethnicity," *Ethnicity*.

25. Andrew Greeley, "The Ethnic Miracle," *The Public Interest* 45 (1976): 20–36.

26. Milton Gordon, *Assimilation in American Life* (New York: Oxford University Press, 1964), pp. 66–81.

27. van den Berghe, *Race and Racism*.

28. Samuel Bowles and Herbert Gintis, *Schooling in Capitalist America* (New York: Basic, 1976); Ogbu, *Minority Education and Caste*.

29. Thomas Sowell, *Black Education: Myths and Tragedies* (New York: McKay, 1972); D. Selakovich, *Ethnicity and the Schools* (Danville, Ill.: Interstate, 1978).

30. Orlando Patterson, "On Guilt, Relativism, and Black-White Relations," *American Scholar* 43 (1973–1974): 122–132.

31. American Association of Colleges for Teacher Education, "No One Model American."

32. R. P. Wolff, "Beyond Tolerance," in *A Critique of Pure Tolerance*, ed. R. P. Wolff, B. Moore, and H. Marcuse (Boston: Beacon, 1975), p. 22.

33. Pratte, "Cultural Diversity and Education."

34. Wolff, "Beyond Tolerance," pp. 18–20.

35. Ibid., p. 50.
36. Robin M. Williams, *American Society*, 3rd ed. (New York: Knopf, 1970), p. 606.
37. Daniel Yankelovich, Inc., "New Portrait of Black America," *Ebony*, September 1973.
38. William J. Wilson, *The Declining Significance of Race* (Chicago: University of Chicago Press, 1978).
39. For a discussion of these cross-ties, see the numerous articles in "The Black Middle Class," *Ebony*, August 1973 (special issue).
40. Wolff, "Beyond Tolerance."
41. James Banks, "The Implications of Multicultural Education for Teacher Education," in *Pluralism and the American Teacher*, ed. F. Klassen and D. Gollnick (Washington, D.C.: American Association of Colleges for Teacher Education, Ethnic Heritage Center for Teacher Education, 1977). Other descriptions of multicultural programs may be found in W. Hunter, ed., *Multicultural Education Through Competency-based Teacher Education* (Washington, D.C.: American Association of Colleges for Teacher Education, 1974).
42. Nathan Glazer, "Cultural Pluralism: The Social Aspect," in *Pluralism in a Democratic Society*, ed. M. Tumin and W. Plotch (New York: Praeger, 1977), p. 24.
43. See, for instance, "California Becoming a New Melting Pot," *New York Times* 22 August 1981.

Chapter 7: Education and Tolerance in the 1980s

1. For detailed reports and analyses of most of these topics, the reader is urged to review the national print media for the period January 1981–May 1982. The principal source used in the present discussion is the *New York Times*.
2. The ensuing discussion of Minimum Competency Testing is based primarily on articles published in two sources: *Phi Delta Kappan*, May 1978 (special issue), and R. Jaeger and C. Title, eds., *Minimum Competency Achievement Testing* (Berkeley: McCutchan, 1980).
3. James Coleman et al., *Equality of Educational Opportunity* (Washington, D.C.: U.S. Government Printing Office, 1966).
4. James Coleman, S. Kilgore and T. Hoffer, *Public and Private Schools*, draft report to the National Center for Educational Statis-

tics, March 1981, p. xxviii. Washington, D.C.: Educational Resources Information Center (ERIC), ED 197 503, unpublished.

5. Arthur Goldberger, "Coleman Goes Private (In Public)," (unpublished) (Madison, Wis., 1981); "Responses of Scholars to the Coleman Report," *School Research Forum*, April 1981, pp. 21–35.

6. "Why Public Schools Are Flunking," *Newsweek*, April 20, 1981, pp. 62–73.

7. U.S., Bureau of the Census, *Statistical Abstract of the United States: 1979*, 100th ed. (Washington, D.C.: U.S., Bureau of the Census, 1979), table 213, p. 136.

8. Ibid, table 218, p. 139.

9. "Why Public Schools Are Flunking."

10. U.S., Bureau of the Census, *Statistical Abstract of the United States: 1979*, table 242, p. 151.

11. Virgina Nordin and William Turner, "More Than Segregation Academies: The Growing Protestant Fundamentalist Schools," *Phi Delta Kappan*, 61 (1980): 391–394.

12. Stephen Steinberg, *The Ethnic Myth* (New York: Atheneum, 1981), p. 54.

13. Relevant rulings of the U.S. Supreme Court include Abington v. Schempp, 374 U.S. 203 (1963), and Engel v. Vitale, 370 U.S. 421 (1962).

14. Coleman et al., *Public and Private Schools*, p. xxiv.

15. Goldberger, "Coleman Goes Private."

16. "School Study Said to Fail to Emphasize Main Point," *New York Times*, 12 April 1981.

17. U.S., Bureau of the Census, *Statistical Abstract of the United States: 1981* (Washington, D.C.: U.S., Bureau of the Census, 1981), table 737, p. 442.

18. Urie Bronfenbrenner, *Two Worlds of Childhood* (New York: Simon & Schuster, 1970); J. Coleman et al., *Youth: Transition to Adulthood*, Report of the Panel on Youth of the President's Science Advisory Committee (Chicago: University of Chicago Press, 1974).

19. "*Minority Report,*" *Wall Street Journal* 29 September 1980.

Bibliography

Adelson, Joseph, and O'Neill, Robert. "Growth of Political Ideas in Adolescence: The Sense of Community." *Journal of Personality and Social Psychology* 4 (1966): 295–306.

Adorno, T. W., Frenkel-Brunswik, E., Levinson, D., and Sanford, R. *The Authoritarian Personality*. New York: Harper & Row, 1950.

Allport, Gordon. *The Nature of Prejudice*. Reading, Mass.: Addison-Wesley, 1954.

Almond, Gabriel, and Verba, Stanley. *The Civic Culture*. Boston: Little, Brown, 1965.

American Association of Colleges for Teacher Education. "No One Model American." *Journal of Teacher Education* 24 (1973): 264–265.

Amir, Yehuda. "The Role of Intergroup Contact in Change of Prejudice and Ethnic Relations." In *Toward the Elimination of Racism*, edited by P. Katz. New York: Pergamon, 1976.

Anderson, Barry. "School Bureaucratization and Alienation from the High School." *Sociology of Education* 46 (1973): 315–334.

Aronson, Elliot, Bridgeman, Diane, and Gefner, Robert. "The Effects of a Cooperative Classroom Structure on Student Behavior and Attitudes." In *Social Psychology of Education*, edited by D. Bar-Tal and L. Saxe. Washington, D.C.: Hemisphere, 1978.

Bachrach, Peter. *The Theory of Democratic Elitism: A Critique*. Boston: Little, Brown, 1968.

Baldwin, Clara, and Baldwin, Alfred. "Personality and Social Development of Handicapped Children." In *Readings in Special Education, 1978–79*. Guilford, Conn.: Special Learning Corp., 1978.

Banks, James. "The Implications of Multicultural Education for Teacher Education." In *Pluralism and the American Teacher*, edited by F. Klassen and D. Gollnick. Washington, D.C.: American Association of Colleges for Teacher Education, Ethnic Heritage Center for Teacher Education, 1977.

Bennett, Christine. "A Case for Pluralism in the Schools." *Phi Delta Kappan* 62 (1981): 589–591.

———. "Interracial Acceptance in Desegregated Schools." *Phi Delta Kappan* 60 (1979): 683–684.

Bettelheim, Bruno, and Janowitz, Morris. *Social Change and Prejudice*. New York: Free Press, 1964.

"The Black Middle Class." *Ebony*, August 1973 (special issue).

Bossert, Steven. *Tasks and Social Relationships in Classrooms*. Cambridge: Cambridge University Press, 1979.

Bowles, Samuel, and Gintis, Herbert. *Schooling in Capitalist America*. New York: Basic, 1976.

Braddock, Jomills. "The Perpetuation of Segregation Across Levels of Education: A Behavioral Assessment of the Contact Hypothesis." *Sociology of Education* 53 (1980): 178–186.

Brant, Irving. *The Bill of Rights: Its Origin and Meaning*. New York: Mentor, 1965.

Breer, Paul, and Locke, Edwin. *Task Experience as a Source of Attitudes*. Homewood, Ill.: Dorsey, 1965.

Bronfenbrenner, Urie. *Two Worlds of Childhood*. New York: Simon & Schuster, 1970.

Carithers, Martha. "School Desegregation and Racial Cleavage, 1954–1970: A Review of the Literature." *Journal of Social Issues* 26, no. 4 (1970): 25–47.

Chesler, Mark. "Contemporary Sociological Theories of Racism." In *Toward the Elimination of Racism*, edited by P. Katz. New York: Pergamon, 1976.

Clement, Dorothy, Eisenhart, Margaret, and Harding, Joe C. "Social-race Relations in a Southern Desegregated School." In *Desegregated Schools: Appraisals of an American Experiment*, edited by R. Rist. New York: Academic. 1979.

Cohen, Elizabeth. "The Effects of Desegregation on Race Relations." *Law and Contemporary Problems* 39 (1975): 271–299.

Coleman, James. *The Adolescent Society*. New York: Free Press, 1961.

Coleman, James, et al. *Youth: Transition to Adulthood*. Report of the Panel on Youth of the President's Science Advisory Committee. Chicago: University of Chicago Press, 1974.

Coleman, James, et al. *Equality of Educational Opportunity*. Washington, D.C.: U.S. Government Printing Office, 1966.

Coleman, James, Kilgore, Sally, and Hoffer, Thomas. *Public and Private Schools*. Draft report to the National Center for Educational Statistics. Washington, D.C.: Educational Resources Information Center (ERIC), ED 197 503, unpublished.

Collins, Thomas. "From Courtrooms to Classrooms: Managing School Desegregation in a Deep South High School." In *Desegre-*

gated Schools: Appraisals of an American Experiment, edited by R. Rist. New York: Academic, 1979.

Commager, Henry Steele. "Our Schools Have Kept Us Free." *Life*, October 16, 1950.

Connor, Frances, Rusalem, Herbert, and Cruickshank, William. "Psychological Considerations of Crippled Children." In *Psychology of Exceptional Children and Youth*, edited by W. Cruickshank. Englewood Cliffs, N.J.: Prentice-Hall, 1971.

Cook, J. William, and Wollersheim, Janet. "The Effect of Labeling of Special Education Students on the Perceptions of Contact Versus Noncontact Normal Peers." *Journal of Special Education* 10 (1976): 187–198.

Coser, Lewis. *Masters of Sociological Thought*. 2nd ed. New York: Harcourt Brace Jovanovich, 1977.

Cremin, Lawrence. *The Republic and the School: Horace Mann on the Education of Free Men*. New York: Teachers College Press, 1957.

Dahl, Robert. *Pluralist Democracy in the United States: Conflict and Consensus*. Chicago: Rand McNally, 1967.

Daniel Yankelovich, Inc. "New Portrait of Black America." *Ebony*, September 1973.

Davidson, Florence. "Respect for Persons and Ethnic Prejudice in Childhood: A Cognitive-developmental Prescription." In *Pluralism in a Democratic Society*, edited by M. Tumin and W. Plotch. New York: Praeger, 1977.

Davis, James. "Communism, Conformity, Cohorts, and Categories: American Tolerance in 1954 and 1972–73." *American Journal of Sociology* 81 (1975): 491–513.

Dawson, Richard, and Prewitt, Kenneth. *Political Socialization*. Boston: Little, Brown, 1969.

Deutscher, Irwin. *What We Say/What We Do*. Glenview, Ill.: Scott, Foresman, 1973.

———. "Words and Deeds: Social Science and Social Policy." *Social Problems* 13 (1966): 235–254.

DeVries, David, and Edwards, Keith. "Student Teams and Learning Games: Their Effects on Cross-race and Cross-sex Interaction." *Journal of Educational Psychology* 66 (1974): 741–749.

Dewey, John. *Democracy and Education*. New York: Free Press, 1966.

Dreeben, Robert. *On What Is Learned in School*. Reading, Mass.: Addison-Wesley, 1968.

Dunn, Lloyd. "Special Education for the Mildly Retarded: Is Much of

It Justifiable?" *Exceptional Children* 35 (1968): 5–22.

Durkheim, Emile. *Education and Sociology*. Glencoe, Ill.: Free Press, 1956.

———. *Moral Education*. New York: Free Press, 1962.

Dye, Thomas, and Zeigler, L. Harmon. *The Irony of Democracy*. 2nd ed. Belmont, Calif.: Duxbury, 1972.

Easton, D. *A Systems Analysis of Political Life*. New York: Wiley, 1965.

Easton, David, and Hess, Robert. "The Child's Political World." *Midwest Journal of Political Science* 6 (1962): 229–246.

Ehman, Lee. "The American School in the Political Socialization Process." *Review of Educational Research* 50 (1980): 99–119.

———. "An Analysis of the Relationships of Selected Educational Variables with the Political Socialization of High School Students." *American Educational Research Journal* 6 (1969): 559–580.

Feldman, Kenneth, and Newcomb, Theodore. *The Impact of College on Students*. San Francisco: Jossey-Bass, 1969.

Ferrar, Jane. "The Dimensions of Tolerance." *Pacific Sociological Review* 19 (1976): 63–81.

Frederick, Robert. *The Third Curriculum*. New York: Appleton, 1959.

Gaertner, Samuel. "Nonreactive Measures in Racial Attitudes Research: A Focus on 'Liberals.'" In *Toward the Elimination of Racism*, edited by P. Katz. New York: Pergamon, 1976.

Gallup, George. "The Eleventh Annual Gallup Poll of the Public's Attitudes Towards the Public Schools." *Phi Delta Kappan* 61 (1979): 33–45.

Gay, Geneva. "Curriculum for Multicultural Teacher Education." In *Pluralism and the American Teacher*, edited by F. Klassen and D. Gollnick. Washington, D.C.: American Association of Colleges for Teacher Education, Ethnic Heritage Center for Teacher Education 1977.

Gearhart, Bill, and Weishahn, Mel. *The Handicapped Child in the Regular Classroom*. St. Louis: Mosby, 1976.

Gerard, Harold, and Miller, Norman. *School Desegregation*. New York: Plenum, 1975.

Gibbs, John. "Kohlberg's Stages of Moral Judgment: A Constructive Critique." In *Stage Theories of Cognitive and Moral Development: Criticisms and Applications*. Harvard Educational Review Reprint no. 13, 1978.

Giles, Raymond, and Gollnick, Donna. "Ethnic/cultural Diversity as Reflected in State and Federal Educational Legislation and Policies." In *Pluralism and the American Teacher*, edited by F. Klassen and D. Gollnick. Washington, D.C.: American Association of Colleges for Teacher Education, Ethnic Heritage Center for Teacher Education, 1977.

Gilhool, Thomas. "Changing Public Policies: Roots and Forces." *Minnesota Education* 2 (1976): 8–14.

Glazer, N. *Affirmative Discrimination*. New York: Basic, 1978.

———. "Cultural Pluralism: The Social Aspect." In *Pluralism in a Democratic Society*, edited by M. Tumin and W. Plotch. New York: Praeger, 1977.

Glazer, Nathan, and Moynihan, Daniel Patrick, eds. *Ethnicity*. Cambridge, Mass.: Harvard University Press, 1975.

Goldberger, Arthur. "Coleman Goes Private (In Public)." Unpublished. Madison, Wis., 1981.

Goldenson, Dennis. "An Alternative View about the Role of the Secondary School in Political Socialization." *Theory and Research in Social Education* 6 (1978): 44–72.

Goodman, Leroy. "A Bill of Rights for the Handicapped." In *Readings in Special Education, 1978–79*. Guilford, Conn.: Special Learning Corp., 1978.

Gordon, C. Wayne. *The Social System of the High School*. Glencoe, Ill.: Free Press, 1957.

Gordon, Milton. *Assimilation in American Life*. New York: Oxford University Press, 1964.

———. "Toward a General Theory of Racial and Ethnic Group Relations." In *Ethnicity*, edited by N. Glazer and D. P. Moynihan. Cambridge, Mass.: Harvard University Press, 1975.

Goslin, David. *The School in Contemporary Society*. Glenview, Ill.: Scott, Foresman, 1965.

Gottlieb, Jay, Semmel, Melvyn, and Veldman, Donald. "Correlates of Social Status Among Mainstreamed Mentally Retarded Children." *Journal of Educational Psychology* 70 (1978): 396–405.

Gracey, Harry. "Learning the Student Role: Kindergarten as Academic Boot Camp." In *The Sociology of Education: A Source Book*, edited by H. Stub. 3rd ed. Homewood, Ill.: Dorsey, 1975.

Greeley, Andrew. "The Ethnic Miracle." *The Public Interest* 45 (1976): 20–36.

Greer, Colin. *The Great School Legend*. New York: Viking, 1972.

Hallahan, Daniel, and Kauffman, James. *Exceptional Children: Introduction to Special Education*. Englewood Cliffs, N.J.: Prentice-Hall, 1978.

Hollingshead, A. B. *Elmstown's Youth*. New York: Wiley, 1949.

Hunter, William, ed. *Multicultural Education Through Competency-based Teacher Education*. Washington, D.C.: American Association of Colleges for Teacher Education, 1974.

Husock, Howard. "Boston: The Problem That Won't Go Away." *New York Times Magazine*, 25 November 1979, p. 32.

Hyman, Herbert, and Wright, Charles. *Education's Lasting Influence on Values*. Chicago: University of Chicago Press, 1979.

Isaacs, Harold. "Basic Group Identity: The Idols of the Tribe." In *Ethnicity*, edited by N. Glazer and D. P. Moynihan. Cambridge, Mass.: Harvard University Press, 1975.

Jackson, Phillip. *Life in Classrooms*. New York: Holt, Rinehart & Winston, 1968.

Jaeger, Richard, and Tittle, Carol, eds. *Minimum Competency Achievement Testing*. Berkeley: McCutchan, 1980.

Jaquet, Constant, ed. *Yearbook of American and Canadian Churches, 1980*. Nashville: Abingdon, 1980.

Jennings, M. Kent, Ehman, Lee, and Niemi, Richard. "Social Studies Teachers and Their Pupils." In *The Political Character of Adolescence*, edited by M. K. Jennings and R. Niemi. Princeton, N.J.: Princeton University Press, 1974.

Jennings, M. Kent, Langton, Kenneth, and Niemi, Richard. "Effects of the High School Civics Curriculum." In *The Political Character of Adolescence*, edited by M. K. Jennings and R. Niemi. Princeton, N.J.: Princeton University Press, 1974.

Johnson, Roger, Rynders, J., Johnson, D., Schmidt, B., and Haider, I. "Interaction Between Handicapped and Nonhandicapped Teenagers as a Function of Situational Goal Structuring: Implications for Mainstreaming." *American Educational Research Journal* 16 (1979): 161–167.

Kallen, Horace. *Culture and Democracy in the United States*. New York: Boni and Liveright, 1924.

Karabel, Jerome, and Halsey, A. H. *Power and Ideology in Education*. New York: Oxford University Press, 1977.

Katz, Phyllis. "Attitude Change in Children: Can the Twig be Straightened?" In *Toward the Elimination of Racism*, edited by P. Katz. New York: Pergamon, 1976.

Kohlberg, Lawrence. "Stage and Sequence: The Cognitive-developmental Approach to Socialization." In *Handbook of Socialization Theory and Research*, edited by D. Goslin. Chicago: Rand McNally, 1969.

Krug, Mark. *The Melting of the Ethnics.* Bloomington, Ind.: Phi Delta Kappa, 1976.

Kuhn, T. *The Structure of Scientific Revolutions.* Chicago: University of Chicago Press, 1963.

Langton, Kenneth. *Political Socialization.* New York: Oxford University Press, 1969.

Langton, Kenneth, and Jennings, M. Kent. "Political Socialization and the High School Civics Curriculum in the United States." *American Political Science Review* 62 (1968): 852–867.

LaPiere, Richard. "Attitudes v. Actions." *Social Forces* 13 (1934): 230–237.

Lasch, Christopher. *The Culture of Narcissism.* New York: Norton, 1979.

Lee, Gordon C. *Crusade Against Ignorance: Thomas Jefferson on Education.* New York: Teachers College Press, 1961.

Levin, Martin. "Social Climates and Political Socialization." In *Learning About Politics*, edited by R. Sigel. New York: Random House, 1970.

Lincoln, James, and Zeitz, Gerard. "Organizational Properties from Aggregate Data: Separating Individual from Structural Effects." *American Sociological Review* 45 (1980): 391–408.

Lipset, Seymour M., and Raab, Earl. *The Politics of Unreason.* New York: Harper & Row, 1970.

Litt, Edgar. "Civic Education, Community Norms, and Political Indoctrination." *American Sociological Review* 28 (1963): 69–75.

McCloskey, Herbert. "Consensus and Ideology in American Politics." *American Political Science Review* 58 (1964): 361–382.

Massialas, Byron. *Education and the Political System.* Reading, Mass.: Addison-Wesley, 1969.

Merelman, Richard. *Political Socialization and Educational Climates.* New York: Holt, Rinehart & Winston, 1971.

Merton, Robert. "Fact and Factitiousness in Ethnic Opinionnaires." *American Sociological Review* 5 (1940): 13–28.

———. *Social Theory and Social Structure.* London: Free Press, 1964.

Milofsky, David. "Schooling the Kids No One Wants." *New York Times Magazine*, January 2, 1977, p. 12.

"Minimum Competency Testing." *Phi Delta Kappan*, May 1978 (special issue).

Montero, Darrel. "Support for Civil Liberties Among a Cohort of High School Graduates and College Students." *Journal of Social*

Issues 31, no. 2 (1975): 123–136.

Morgan, Edward. *Inequality in Classroom Learning*. New York: Praeger, 1977.

Myrdahl, Gunnar. *An American Dilemma*. New York: Harper & Row, 1954.

National Center for Educational Statistics. *The Condition of Education, 1976 Edition*. Washington, D.C.: U.S. Government Printing Office, 1976.

Neilsen, H. Dean. *Tolerating Political Dissent*. Stockholm: Almqvist & Wiksell, 1977.

Newman, William. *American Pluralism*. New York: Harper & Row, 1973.

Nordin, Virginia, and Turner, William. "More Than Segregation Academies: The Growing Protestant Fundamentalist Schools." *Phi Delta Kappan* 61 (1981): 391–394.

Novak, Michael. *The Rise of the Unmeltable Ethnics*. New York: Macmillan, 1971.

Nunn, Clyde, Crockett, Harry, and Williams, J. Allen. *Tolerance for Non-Conformity*. San Francisco: Jossey-Bass, 1978.

Odetola, Theophilus, Erickson, Edsel, Bryan, Clifford E., and Walker, Lewis. "Organizational Structure and Student Alienation." *Educational Administration Quarterly* 8 (1972): 15–26.

Ogbu, John. *Minority Education and Caste*. New York: Academic, 1977.

Orfield, Gary. "How to Make Desegregation Work: The Adaptation of Schools to Their Newly-integrated Student Bodies." *Law and Contemporary Problems* 39 (1975): 314–340.

Parsons, Talcott. "The School Class as a Social System." *Harvard Educational Review* 29 (1959): 297–318.

———. *The Social System*. Glencoe, Ill.: Free Press, 1951.

———. "Some Theoretical Considerations on the Nature and Trends of Change in Ethnicity." In *Ethnicity*, edited by N. Glazer and D. Moynihan. Cambridge, Mass.: Harvard University Press, 1977.

Patchen, Martin, Davidson, James, Hoffman, Gerhard and Brown, William. "Determinants of Students' Interracial Behavior and Opinion Change." *Sociology of Education* 50 (1977): 55–75.

Patrick, John. "Political Socialization and Political Education in the Schools." In *Handbook of Political Socialization: Theory and Research*, edited by S. Renshon. New York: Free Press, 1977.

Patterson, Orlando. "On Guilt, Relativism, and Black-white Relations." *American Scholar* 43 (1973): 122–133.

Paul, James, Turnbull, Ann, and Cruickshank, William. *Mainstreaming: A Practical Guide*. Syracuse: Syracuse University Press, 1977.

Pederson, Eigel, and Faucher, Therese A., with Eaton, William. "A New Perspective on the Effects of First-grade Teachers on Children's Subsequent Adult Status." *Harvard Educational Review* 48 (1978): 1–31.

Pennings, Johannes. "Measures of Organizational Structure: A Methodological Note." *American Journal of Sociology* 79 (1973): 686–704.

Pettigrew, Thomas. "Racially Separate or Together." *Journal of Social Issues* 25, no. 1 (1969): 43–69.

Pratte, Richard. "Cultural Diversity and Education." In *Ethics and Educational Policy*, edited by K. Strike and K. Egan. London: Routledge & Kegan Paul, 1978.

Proshansky, Harold. "The Development of Intergroup Attitudes," In *Review of Child Development Research*, edited by L. W. Hoffman and M. L. Hoffman. New York: Russell Sage Foundation, 1966.

Protho, James, and Grigg, Charles. "Fundamental Principles of Democracy: Bases of Agreement and Disagreement." *Journal of Politics* 22 (1960): 276–294.

Rafalides, Madelaine, and Hoy, Wayne. "Student Sense of Alienation and Pupil Control Orientation of High Schools." *High School Journal* 55 (1971): 101–111.

Ravitch, Diane. *The Revisionists Revised*. New York: Basic, 1978.

Read, Frank. "Judicial Evolution of the Law of School Integration Since Brown v. Board of Education." *Law and Contemporary Problems* 39 (1975): 7–49.

Renshon, Stanley. "Assumptive Frameworks in Political Socialization Theory." In *Handbook of Political Socialization: Theory and Research*, edited by S. Renshon. New York: Free Press, 1977.

Reynolds, Maynard, and Rosen, Sylvia. "Special Education: Past, Present, and Future." In *Readings in Special Education, 1978–79*. Guilford, Conn.: Special Learning, 1978.

Rist, Ray C. "Student Social Class and Teacher Expectations: The Self-fulfilling Prophecy in Ghetto Education." *Harvard Educational Review* 40 (1970): 411–451.

Roemer, Joseph, and Allen, Charles. *Extra-curricular Activities in Junior and Senior High Schools*. New York: Heath, 1926.

Rokeach, Milton. "Attitudes: The Nature of Attitudes." In *International Encyclopedia of the Social Sciences*, vol. 16. New York: Macmillan and Free Press, 1968.

Ryan, William. *Blaming the Victim*. New York: Random House, 1971.

St. John, Nancy. *School Desegregation: Outcomes for Children*. New York: Wiley, 1975.

Schofield, Janet. "School Desegregation and Intergroup Relations." In *Social Psychology of Education*, edited by D. Bar-Tal and L. Saxe. Washington, D.C.: Hemisphere, 1978.

Schofield, Janet, and Sagar, H. Andrew. "The Social Context of Learning in an Interracial School." In *Desegregated Schools: Appraisals of an American Experiment*, edited by R. Rist. New York: Academic, 1979.

Selakovitch, Daniel. *Ethnicity and the Schools*. Danville, Ill.: Interstate, 1978.

Selznick, Gertrude, and Steinberg, Stephen. *The Tenacity of Prejudice*. New York: Harper & Row, 1969.

Serow, Robert, and Solomon, Daniel. "Classroom Climates and Students' Intergroup Behavior." *Journal of Educational Psychology* 71 (1979): 669–676.

Serow, Robert, and Strike, Kenneth. "Students' Attitudes Towards High School Governance: Implications for Social Education." *Theory and Research in Social Education* 6, no. 3 (1978): 12–26.

Simpson, George, and Yinger, J. Milton. *Racial and Cultural Minorities*, 4th ed. New York: Harper & Row, 1972.

Sowell, Thomas. *Black Education: Myths and Tragedies*. New York: McKay, 1972.

Steinberg, Stephen. *The Ethnic Myth*. New York: Atheneum, 1981.

Stent, Madelon, Hazard, William, and Rivlin, Harry. *Cultural Pluralism in Education*. New York: Appleton, Century-Crofts, 1973.

Stouffer, Samuel. *Communism, Conformity, and Civil Liberties*. New York: Doubleday, 1955.

Suchman, Edward, Dean, John, and Williams, Robin M. *Desegregation: Some Propositions and Research Suggestions*. New York: Anti-defamation League of B'nai Brith, 1958.

Tapp, June, and Kohlberg, Lawrence. "Developing Senses of Law and Legal Justice." *Journal of Social Issues* 27 (1971): 65–92.

Tesconi, Charles. *Schooling in America*. Boston: Houghton Mifflin, 1975.

Tocqueville, Alexis de. *Democracy in America*, vol. I. New York: Colonial, 1899.

Torney, Judith. "Socialization of Attitudes Toward the Legal System." *Journal of Social Issues* 27 (1971): 137–154.

Torney, Judith, Oppenheim, A., and Farnen, Russell F. *Civic Education in Ten Countries*. New York: Wiley, 1975.

Trow, Martin. "Small Businessmen, Political Tolerance, and Support for McCarthy." *American Journal of Sociology* 54 (1958): 270–281.

Tumin, Melvin. Introduction to *Pluralism in a Democratic Society*, edited by M. Tumin and W. Plotch. New York: Praeger, 1977.

U.S., Bureau of Education. *Cardinal Principles of Secondary Education*. Bulletin no. 35. Washington, D.C.: Department of the Interior, 1918. Reprinted in F. Roubinger, H. Rowe, L. Piper, and K. West, eds. *The Development of Secondary Education*. London: Macmillan, 1969.

U.S., Bureau of the Census. *Statistical Abstract of the United States: 1979*. 100th ed. Washington, D.C.: U.S., Bureau of the Census, 1979.

U.S., Bureau of the Census. *Statistical Abstract of the United States*, 1981. 102nd ed. Washington, D.C.: U.S., Bureau of the Census, 1981.

U.S., Commission on Civil Rights. *Fulfilling the Letter and the Spirit of the Law*. Washington, D.C.: U.S., Commission on Civil Rights, 1976.

————. *Racial Isolation in the Public Schools*. Washington, D.C.: U.S., Commission on Civil Rights, 1967.

U.S., Department of Health, Education, and Welfare. *Progress Toward a Free, Appropriate Public Education*. Washington, D.C.: U.S., Government Printing Office, 1979.

van den Berghe, Pierre. *Race and Racism: A Comparative Perspective*. 2nd ed. New York: Wiley, 1978.

Violas, Paul. *The Training of the Urban Working Class*. Chicago: Rand McNally, 1978.

Waller, Willard. *The Sociology of Teaching*. New York: Wiley, 1967.

Wayland, Sloan. "Interrelationship Between School Districts." In *The School in Society*, edited by S. Sieber and D. Wilder. New York: Free Press, 1973.

Weigel, Russell, Wiser, Patricia, and Cook, Stuart. "The Impact of Cooperative Learning Experiences on Cross-ethnic Relations and Attitudes." *Journal of Social Issues* 31 (1975): 229–244.

Weinberg, Meyer. *A Chance to Learn*. Cambridge: Cambridge University Press, 1977.

"Why Public Schools Are Flunking." *Newsweek*, April 20, 1981, pp. 62–73.

Wicker, Allan. "Attitudes v. Actions: The Relationship of Verbal and Overt Behavioral Responses to Attitude Objects." *Journal of Social Issues* 25, no. 4 (1969): 41–78.

Williams, Robin M. *American Society*. 3rd ed. New York: Knopf, 1970.

————. *Mutual Accommodation*. Minneapolis: University of Minnesota Press, 1977.

————. *The Reduction of Intergroup Tensions*. New York: Social Science Research Council, 1947.

————. *Strangers Next Door*. Englewood Cliffs, N.J.: Prentice-Hall, 1964.

————. "Values: The Concept of Values." In *International Encyclopedia of the Social Sciences*, vol. 16. New York: Macmillan and Free Press, 1968.

Wilson, William J. *The Declining Significance of Race*. Chicago: University of Chicago Press, 1978.

Wolff, Robert P. "Beyond Tolerance." In *A Critique of Pure Tolerance*, edited by R. P. Wolff, B. Moore, and H. Marcuse. Boston: Beacon, 1975.

Zelder, Empress. "Public Opinion and Public Education for the Handicapped Child—Court Decisions 1873–1950." *Exceptional Children* 19 (1953): 187–198.

Zellman, Gail. "Antidemocratic Beliefs: A Survey and Some Explanations." *Journal of Social Issues* 31 (1975) 31–54.

Zellman, Gail, and Sears, David. "Childhood Origins of Tolerance for Dissent." *Journal of Social Issues* 27, no. 1 (1971): 109–136.

Index